FOOTBALL'S
STRANGEST®
MATCHES

Other titles in the STRANGEST series

Law's Strangest Cases
London's Strangest Tales
Rugby's Strangest Matches

Titles coming soon

Cricket's Strangest Matches
Golf's Strangest Rounds
Kent's Strangest Tales
Medicine's Strangest Cases
Motor-racing's Strangest Races
Running's Strangest Tales
Shakespeare's Strangest Tales
Teachers' Strangest Tales
Tennis's Strangest Matches

FOOTBALL'S STRANGEST® MATCHES

Extraordinary but true stories
from over a century of football

ANDREW WARD

PORTICO

Published in the United Kingdom in 2016 by
Portico
1 Gower Street
London
WC1E 6HD

An imprint of Pavilion Books Company Ltd

ISBN 978-1-91023-286-6

A CIP catalogue record for this book is available from the British Library.

10 9 8 7 6 5 4 3 2 1

Reproduction by Colourdepth UK
Printed and bound by Bookwell, Finland

This book can be ordered direct from the publisher at www.pavilionbooks.com

CONTENTS

INTRODUCTION   10

THE CROSSBAR PROTEST (1888)   13

THE MYSTERY GAME (1889)   14

THE ONE-MAN TEAM (1891)   15

THE TRUSTED GOALKEEPER (1892)   17

THE GAME OF THREE HALVES (1894)   20

THE FOUR-MINUTE GAME (1894)   22

NOT ONE SHOT AT GOAL (1898)   23

COMPLETED – 15 WEEKS LATER (1898–9)   26

THE PENALTY-KICKING ELEPHANT (LATE 1890s)   29

A TEMPESTUOUS SEMI-FINAL (1899)   30

SOCCER SICKNESS (1902)   32

FISHERMEN VS FIREMEN (1905)   34

UNDER THE SCORCHING SUN (1906)   35

THE CIRCUS GAME (1910)   38

THE 'TONYPANDEMONIUM' GAME (1910)   39

THE ELECTION CAMPAIGN GAME (1910)   40

DEATH OF A REFEREE (1912)   42

BATTLE AT HALF-TIME (1912)	43
THE TEAM AWARDED FOUR PENALTIES (1913)	45
THE WAR GAME (1914)	47
ONE-ARMED MEN VS WOMEN (1917)	48
SOCCER IN GAS MASKS (1917–18)	50
WILFRED MINTER'S GOALSCORING FEAT (1922)	52
EXPERIMENTING WITH THE RULES (1925)	55
STRIKERS AGAINST POLICE (1926)	57
AMATEURS VS PROFESSIONALS (1926)	59
INTRODUCING THE EIGHT-SQUARE GAME (1927)	60
EIGHT ON A DEBUT (1930)	62
EXPOSING CHELSEA'S DEFENCE (1931)	64
THE FASTEST INDIVIDUAL GOALS (1931)	67
SIX IN 21 MINUTES (1932)	69
THE GAME WITH TWO REFEREES (1935)	70
'AVALANCHE AT ASTON' (1935)	72
TEN GOALS AT HIS FIRST ATTEMPT (1936)	74
TAKING IT AT WALKING PACE (1937)	75
A MATTER OF CLASS (1938)	77
FREAKISH AND GOALFUL (1941)	79
FARCE IN THE FOG (1945)	81
THE 203-MINUTE GAME (1946)	83
WHEN TWO PLAYERS DIED (1948)	85
DAYLIGHT ROBBERY (1949)	87
'FOOTBALL'S MOST AMAZING EXPERIMENT' (1949)	89
THE INVISIBLE GAME (1950)	91

TWO TEAMS, ONE MANAGER (1952)   94

THE 44-MINUTE GAME (1956)   96

SECOND-HALF TRANSFORMATION (1957)   98

THE TRIPLICATED CUP TIE (1958)   100

GIANT-KILLING GLORY (1959)   102

THE MISSING FUSES (1959)   105

'FANTASTIC, INCREDIBLE, AMAZING' (1960)   107

THE DISALLOWED DOUBLE HAT-TRICK (1961)   109

THE NIGHTMARE DAY-TRIP (1961)   110

FAREWELL IN A BLIZZARD (1962)   112

ALL IN THE IMAGINATION (1963)   114

THE ABANDONED INTERNATIONAL (1963)   117

THE GAME IN TWO GROUNDS (1965)   118

A PAIR OF BROKEN LEGS (1966)   120

THE POPULAR NORTH KOREANS (1966)   122

THE FANTASTIC CHAMPIONSHIP DECIDER (1967)   124

A TOUCH OF MAYHEM (1967)   127

THE REFEREE'S WINNING GOAL (1968)   129

THE SOCCER WAR (1969)   130

SOUTH AMERICAN FREE-FOR-ALL (1971)   134

THE VITAL DISPUTED GOAL (1971)   136

THE HIGH-SCORERS' CUP FINAL (1971)   139

THE ENDLESS CUP TIE (1971)   141

REFEREE WHO FORGOT THE RULES (1971)   144

SIXTEEN MINUTES OF DISBELIEF (1972)   147

CROWD POWER (1974)   150

UNDER THE SPELL (1975)	152
THE 28-PENALTY SHOOT-OUT (1975)	154
OVATION FOR A STREAKER (1975)	156
THE ONE-SCORER FOUR-GOAL DRAW (1976)	158
THE GAME THAT NEVER WAS (1978)	160
WARRING TEAM-MATES (1979)	162
THE FALKLAND ISLANDS GAMES (1970s)	164
A LEGAL PRECEDENT (1980)	165
THE 'ESCAPE TO VICTORY' GAME (1980)	167
BEHIND CLOSED DOORS (1980)	169
THE BROKEN GOALPOST (1981)	171
SETTLED OUT OF COURT (1981)	173
TEAM ON STRIKE (1983)	175
THE MISSING 78 SECONDS (1983)	177
STRANGE SUBSTITUTION (1984)	179
THE 68-HOUR GAME (1984)	181
'WE WANT 20' (1984)	182
A POOCH OF A GOAL (1985)	185
FIVE PENALTIES IN A GAME (1989)	187
A FLARE-UP FOR FIFA (1989)	189
FOOTBALL FOR PIGS (1990)	191
A RE-ENACTMENT GAME (1991)	193
PICKING THE WRONG PLAYERS (1992)	196
'ONE TEAM IN TALLINN' (1996)	199
AS YOU WERE, LADS (1996)	202
WATCHING A DIFFERENT GAME (1998)	204

TENSION AT WEMBLEY (1998)   207

GOALKEEPER'S GOAL SAVES CARLISLE UNITED (1999)   211

SENT-OFF PLAYER SUBSTITUTED (2000)   214

AUSTRALIA 31 AMERICAN SAMOA 0 (2001)   216

REFEREE SCORES WITH SUPERB VOLLEY (2001)   218

34 CONSECUTIVE SHOOT-OUT GOALS (2001)   220

MATCH ABANDONED – TOO FEW PLAYERS (2002)   222

149 OWN GOALS (2002)   226

UK POLITICIANS TAKE ON IRAQ (2004)   228

THE GAME OF 25 HALVES (2004)   230

'DODGY LASAGNE' (2006)   231

THE MATCH IN THE RIVER (2007)   234

POSTPONED (2008)   237

BEACH BALL SCORES WINNING GOAL (2009)   239

ILLOGAN RBL RESERVES 55 MADRON FC 0 (2010)   241

WHEEL POWER FC 58 NOVA 2010 FC 0 (2012)   243

GOALIE SENT OFF ... AGAIN AND AGAIN (2015)   245

A PAIR OF BROKEN ARMS (2015)   247

THE PICK-UP GAME (SAT. AND TUES.)   250

INTRODUCTION

In the beginning they were all strange games. When the first official club – Sheffield, in 1857 – was formed, there were no other teams to play against. So the bachelors played the married men – until a nearby garrison put up a challenge. And one early Sheffield rule stipulated that players must hold half-crown coins while they played – to prevent pushing with the open hand.

In compiling previous editions of this book I tried to avoid such weird evolutionary encounters, opting instead for games played under more formal rules as we know them. Each game was strange in that it provided some new experience for spectators or players. Sometimes people went to a game expecting novelty, as happened with the hypnotist at Hinckley or the New Bedford men against the Preston women. On other occasions one person has made a spectacular impact on the game, whether through failure (like Jimmy Warner of Aston Villa), success (like Wilfred Minter of St Albans City) or a perverse mixture of both (like Chris Nicholl of Aston Villa). But the most obvious candidates for inclusion are those games in which events have simply departed from football tradition and entered a new world, beyond the control of the participants. Who could anticipate a dog heading a goal or a referee scoring the winning goal of a Football League match?

Strangeness, of course, is relative and culturally rooted. Inevitably, this collection is a personal selection. It draws heavily on the British professional scene, the section of soccer history with which I am most familiar, and only occasionally crosses national boundaries. I suspect that there have been even stranger matches around the world, or in the local leagues, well deserving of mention. For instance, I have heard of a player scoring the winning goal without stepping on to the field; apparently, as a substitute, he immediately took a corner-kick and fell over with a broken ankle as the ball curled into the net. And an editor friend, Graham Hart, once asked me how a player could score three goals without any other player touching the ball. The answer, in case you haven't worked it out, is that he scores an own goal, picks the ball out of the net, carries it to the halfway-line, kicks off by angrily punting the ball high in the air and runs after it full-pelt. He is just inside the penalty area when he is tripped, whereupon he grabs the ball (still not touched by anybody else), puts it on the penalty spot, slams it past the goalkeeper, who doesn't touch it, and runs into the net to collect the ball. The referee blows for half-time, so the player hangs on to the ball and his team has the kick-off to start the second half. Once more he punts the ball high in the air and, lo and behold, he is tripped again and scores from another penalty, his third goal without anyone else touching the ball.

Since the first edition of *Football's Strangest Matches* was published, in 1989, people have kindly written to me with suggestions for matches that could have been included. I wish I had known at the time about 'Jockeys vs Boxers' (1913) and the motor-bike football matches of the 1930s. I also wish I had researched the details of St Mirren's 11-day boat trip to play Notts County at Barcelona's new ground in 1922 and West Auckland Town's Sir Thomas Lipton Trophy wins (1909 and 1911). But no book on strange matches can be comprehensive.

Some of the stories in this book, like 'Wilfred Minter's Goalscoring Feat' (1922), have become stranger in the light of the modern game. Other events, such as law cases and protracted penalty shoot-outs, have become more common. In future we may see headlines like 'Law Court Decides Match Result' and 'Penalty Shoot-out Halted by Breakfast'.

Over the years I have updated the book with additional stories but have made only minor changes to the original text. Certain stories could be expanded on the basis of new information. For instance, more is known about 'The War Game' (1914) through books such as *Christmas Truce* by Malcolm Brown and *Der Kleine Frieden im Grossen Krieg* (The Small Peace in the Big War) by Michael Jürgs. And Dan Gordon and Nick Bonner have now told the story of the 1966 North Korea team in their award-winning documentary 'The Game of Their Lives'.

My favourite category of strange matches is still the pick-up game. People of various ages and qualities meet informally on a small patch of land. They divide into roughly even sides, adapt rules if necessary and do their best to maintain some sort of justice without an official referee. The spectators may include a man walking his dog, a passenger on a bus, and a bicycle rider, who wonders if he can join the losing team. Strange matches take place at all levels and I hope they will continue to entertain us.

Andrew Ward

THE CROSSBAR PROTEST

LONDON, DECEMBER 1888

This was the year Crewe Alexandra reached an FA Cup semi-final. Along the way they played a strange match with the Swifts in Kensington.

Crewe progressed to the fourth round (the last 23) by beating Druids and Northwich Victoria. They had a bye in the third round, as would nine clubs in the fourth.

Crewe and the Swifts drew their fourth-round tie 2–2 at Crewe. They replayed on the new Queen's Ground in West Kensington. The Swifts won 3–2, but Crewe protested that the crossbars were at different heights.

'The height of the goal-posts formed the basis of an appeal against the result,' wrote the *Crewe and Nantwich Chronicle*. 'A measurement revealed that they were within a few inches of the specified height.'

The appeal was upheld. The teams had to replay again on a neutral ground, and Crewe beat the Swifts 2–1 at Derby.

After this controversy, the Football Association passed a rule that protests about the ground, markings and goals must be made before the kick-off, not at the end of the game.

Crewe went on to beat Derby County in the fifth round and Middlesbrough in the sixth. Their semi-final opponents were Preston North End, then invincible. The game was played in Liverpool with a lake on the ground. It was really a game of water-polo. Crewe lost 4–0.

THE MYSTERY GAME

SHEFFIELD, AUGUST 1889

An FA Cup semi-final, played at Bramall Lane in 1889, sparked an idea. Several local soccer dignitaries decided to form a football section of the Sheffield United Cricket Club. Bramall Lane was big enough to take cricket and football.

At first it was a club without players. Advertisements in the local newspapers weren't especially successful – three players were acquired. Also, there were the first signs that the new club wouldn't be accepted easily. Sheffield Wednesday were already established. Other Sheffield clubs looked at Sheffield United suspiciously. The new club tactfully recruited outside Sheffield, relying particularly on Scotland. By the end of the summer Sheffield United had a team of assorted players, the best of whom turned out to be Howlett, a bespectacled goalkeeper from Gainsborough.

Sheffield United's first game was a mystery game. Whether they were expecting trouble from rival clubs, or the embarrassment of players not fitting in with one another immediately, is unclear. Nevertheless, the club gathered all the new players and sneaked away in a brake without telling anyone where they were going. They reckoned without the Sherlock Holmes qualities of one Sheffield reporter and Sheffield Wednesday captain Ted Brayshaw, both of whom succeeded in following the brake. They were able to reveal later that Sheffield United went to the Hallam Cricket Club where they lost 3–1 to Sheffield Football Club.

THE ONE-MAN TEAM

BURNLEY, DECEMBER 1891

Snow was falling heavily and it was one of the coldest weeks of the year. No one felt much like playing football. Certainly none of the Blackburn Rovers players did; but, being mainly professionals, they came out of the pavilion to take on Burnley.

Conceding three goals in the first 25 minutes did nothing to raise their spirits. Already it was a tetchy game. Two players squared up to each other in a bid to keep warm and settle a quarrel in the cold. When half-time arrived everybody was pleased.

The ten-minute interval passed. Burnley were on the field but there was no sign of Blackburn Rovers. The referee was the notorious J.C. Clegg from Sheffield, a high-ranking FA official and a man to stand no nonsense. Nor did he like waiting in the cold. He warned the teams that he would start in two minutes. In fact he waited four. Even then not all the Rovers players had returned to the pitch.

Soon tempers rose again. The two feuding players came to blows and were sent off. But what followed next was extraordinary. All the Blackburn players except goalkeeper Herby Arthur left the field. The referee, aware that he had done the correct thing by starting the game when there were more than six players, simply carried on. It was Burnley against the opposing goalkeeper.

Herby Arthur was nearing the end of his tremendous

career with Blackburn Rovers. He had joined the club as a right-half in 1880, then volunteered to keep goal in the reserve team when a vacancy occurred with no obvious replacement. He played in Rovers' hat-trick of FA Cup Final wins in the mid-1880s and became an established England international. Unlike most of the Rovers' players, he remained an amateur.

This was his biggest test. Burnley restarted the game and bore down on his goal.

'Offside,' yelled Herby Arthur. It was given.

There followed an eternal period of time-wasting. Herby Arthur, with no one to pass the ball to, dallied as long as he could. Eventually the referee gave up and abandoned the game.

Blackburn Rovers later apologised, saying that their players were numb with cold and couldn't continue. Two days later Herby Arthur was given a benefit when Rovers played Sunderland.

THE TRUSTED GOALKEEPER

LONDON, MARCH 1892

When Aston Villa reached the 1892 FA Cup Final, one of the stars of the team was 27-year-old Jimmy Warner, a fine and trusted goalkeeper, one of the oldest players in the team. Five years earlier, Warner had kept goal so magnificently that many said he had won Villa the FA Cup. Now Villa were 7–4 favourites to win the FA Cup again ... but the bookmakers reckoned without the strangest performance of Jimmy Warner's career.

Villa's short odds for the FA Cup Final were more than justified given their success in the League – they were pressing for the Championship. On the other hand, their Cup Final opponents, West Bromwich Albion, were languishing in the relegation zone.

A week before the Final, Villa flexed their muscles with a 12–2 win against Accrington. Then the team went to Holt Fleet for special training – running exercises, brine-baths at Droitwich and a spell of football practice every afternoon. On the Tuesday, when it snowed, the quick-thinking trainer moved the players into a 70-yard (64-m) boat-shed and continued the preparations under cover.

Already, during this pre-Cup Final week, Jimmy Warner was being noticed. Not by players, or spectators, or the press, but by Villa committee members, who were monitoring their goalkeeper's activities. It was alleged that Warner would not go through the same training schedule as the other players, and that instead of remaining with his team-mates he 'preferred the company of a certain person to whom the committee objected and who had actually been with him at Holt Fleet against the wish of the committee'.

On Cup Final day, there were about 30,000 people at Kennington Oval, some of them perched precariously on top of the mighty gas-holder. Most knew that on paper Aston Villa should win by a street.

In West Brom's first attack Jasper Geddes sent in a screw shot: 'Warner received it, but the ball seemed to spin out of his hands, and the first goal was scored for the Albion only three minutes from the start.'

It was later described in the press as a 'terrible blunder' but it looked likely to be academic when Villa swarmed to the West Brom end. Jimmy Cowan put a free-kick straight into the West Brom goal-net – nets were being used in a Cup Final for the first time – but as nobody touched the ball it didn't count as a goal, such were the rules of the day.

For 20 minutes Villa used the wind to stay on top, then Jimmy Warner had his second chance to shine: 'Warner partly muffed it, and Nicholls rushed up to send it through the posts.' After half-time it was 2–0 to West Brom, against the wind, against the odds.

In the fifty-fifth minute West Brom's 'Baldy' Reynolds shot from 40 yards (36.6m). Warner was hopelessly out of position. 3–0 to Albion.

Although Aston Villa dominated the rest of the game, they could not score. Reporters chose words like 'lamentable exhibition' to describe Jimmy Warner's afternoon's work, and Villa fans started their inquests. Attention switched to the Old College public house at Spring Hill, where Warner was the landlord. That evening supporters sought retribution by smashing all the windows in the pub.

A rumour spread. Warner had lost money on a big sporting bet, so the goalkeeper had thrown the FA Cup Final to recoup his money.

Warner vehemently denied this, saying he had bet £18 to £12 against West Brom winning, and an even £1 on them not scoring. Why would he want his business to suffer, his wife blackguarded and a mob threatening his pub? Show us your proof, declared Warner, who promised to give his accusers a good thrashing if necessary.

The next Wednesday, a few days before a vital League game with Sunderland, Warner failed to show for training. The next set of rumours claimed he had taken flight from his pub with a week's takings and a servant girl.

Fielding a deputy goalkeeper, Villa lost at Sunderland, finished fourth in the League and went down 2–0 to West Brom in the semi-final of the Birmingham Cup.

Jimmy Warner had played his last game for Aston Villa. The next season he showed up briefly with Newton Heath (later called Manchester United), no doubt thankful that not every newspaper had castigated him for his bizarre display in the Cup Final. 'Certainly he did fumble a lot with almost every shot he had to negotiate,' wrote one reporter, 'but I incline to the opinion that his backs were outclassed by the Albion forwards, and he, in consequence, was not so fully supported as he was wont to be.'

Perhaps.

THE GAME OF
THREE HALVES

SUNDERLAND, SEPTEMBER 1894

On the first day of the 1894–5 soccer season Sunderland were at home to Derby County. The official referee, Mr Kirkham, was late. The game started with a deputy in charge, later named as John Conqueror of Southwick. The two teams played for 45 minutes and then Mr Kirkham arrived. What should he do?

Mr Kirkham made an incredible decision. He offered Derby County, who were losing 3–0, the option of starting again. Naturally they took it. Two more halves followed, and the game became known as 'the game of three halves'.

Derby were captained by England international John Goodall, who lost the toss twice. Derby were forced to kick against a strong gale for the first two halves. But the biggest panic was among the pressmen present at the game. They had already despatched messages all over the country to the effect that Sunderland were winning 3–0 at half-time. Fortunately, Derby obliged by conceding three more goals during the second first half.

Perversely, the decision to start the game *de novo* probably favoured Sunderland more than Derby. After kicking against the wind for 90 minutes the visiting players were, to say the least, weary. Sunderland scored five more in the third half. The result was recorded as an 8–0 win although Sunderland had scored 11 goals during the three halves. A pattern was set for the season. Sunderland sailed to their third Football League Championship, while Derby were fortunate to hang on to their First Division status.

The 'game of three halves' assumed a legendary place among the folklore of Derby County players, none more than England-international goalkeeper Jack Robinson, who conceded 11 goals that afternoon. Robinson had previously boasted that he would never concede 10 goals in a game (adding as a joke that he would come out of goal when the opposition reached 9) and his team-mates debated whether the Sunderland game counted as 8 or 11. Robinson explained the débâcle by his failure to eat rice pudding before the match at Sunderland – the only time he missed with his superstition. 'No pudding, no points,' Robinson would tell his team-mates, who would go to great lengths to indulge their temperamental goalkeeper. One day at Burnley, when a hotel waitress announced the rice pudding was 'off', John Goodall went searching for an hour before he came up with a plate of something which would pass for the same dish. Derby County won at Burnley that day, and they played just two halves.

THE FOUR-MINUTE GAME
STOKE, DECEMBER 1894

Referees have discretionary powers to suspend or terminate a game whenever they deem it necessary. In Britain, the reason is usually the weather, although referees are advised to give the matter very careful consideration before yielding to the elements. Otherwise there would be very little soccer played. I know of one Football League game – Grimsby Town against Oldham Athletic in 1909 – where weather conditions twice caused an abandonment. Over a period of seven weeks these two teams met three times and played almost 220 minutes of soccer. Grimsby won 2–0 after trailing by a goal in the second game.

Among the candidates for the shortest-ever game must be the occasion Stoke City entertained Wolverhampton Wanderers in a blinding snowstorm. The weather was so bad that only about 300 or 400 people turned up to watch. Play immediately proved farcical. The referee, Mr Helme, decided to abandon the game after four minutes (some sources say three). The storm soon cleared but the wind persisted, and the conditions were unbearable for spectators and players. For the record, Stoke won the toss.

NOT ONE SHOT AT GOAL

STOKE, APRIL 1898

Modern-day soccer may have its highly developed defensive strategies and across-the-field build-up, but the strangest shot-shy game of all took place almost 120 years ago, when Stoke City and Burnley engineered a goalless draw to save their places in the First Division.

Stoke and Burnley were engaged with two other teams (Newcastle and Blackburn) in a series of test matches to decide promotion and relegation between the two divisions. On the morning of the final round of matches, Stoke and Burnley were joint top of the mini-league. A draw would suit them both, but it didn't suit the 4,000 people who braved torrential rain and strong wind to attend the game at Stoke's Victoria Ground.

It was a fiasco. The goalkeepers hardly touched the ball, passes went to opponents when either team looked well-placed to attack, and, if a forward did by chance find himself in a shooting position he would aim at the corner-flag. Players' kit remained surprisingly clean in the atrocious conditions, and the best chance of a goal was a tame backpass.

The crowd quickly realised what was happening. They booed and jeered, or, for variation, cheered sarcastically. They shouted kind words of advice.

'Come off the field, we're doing more than you!' 'Play the game!' 'Them goal-nets were invented for a reason.'

As the second half progressed, still no goals, still no shots at goal, the crowd on the Boothen Road side of the ground began to make their own entertainment. When the ball was kicked into their small wooden stand, they hung on to it. To their utter disgust another ball appeared. Undaunted, however, they tried again, and again, and again. This small section of the crowd spent most of the second half trying to stop the game by keeping all the footballs. They put one on top of the grandstand and another in the River Trent. Five balls were used altogether, but the game continued to its bitter goalless end.

The crowd's game within a game did lead to the day's best action. A linesman sprinted along the touchline in a bid to catch a ball before it went into the crowd. A perambulating policeman had his eye on the same ball. The linesman collided with the policeman and they lay spreadeagled across the track. The crowd roared, but only with laughter.

The result was never in doubt. Stoke City retained their First Division status and Burnley were promoted from Division Two. Poor Newcastle United, whose players were showing much more effort in defeating Blackburn, finished third in the mini-league, a point behind Stoke and Burnley.

Perhaps one interesting question is how the goalless draw was arranged such that the players trusted one another. Among the participants were experienced Jimmy Ross, who played in five successive test–match series (for Preston, Liverpool and Burnley), and most interestingly, Jack 'Happy Jack' Hillman, the burly and brilliant Burnley goalkeeper whose career was always within a whisker of controversy and comedy.

Hillman, a Devonian by birth, played for Burnley and Everton before a two-season spell with Dundee. During his second season with the Scottish club Hillman was suspended for not trying, which was why he came to Burnley for £130 in time to help them into the First Division. Hillman was then in his late twenties, but much was still to happen to him. He played a game for England, and was twice suspended by the FA – for a season (1900–1) after allegedly bribing Nottingham Forest players to lose to Burnley, and for eight months (1906–7) for receiving illegal payments as a Manchester City player.

Jack Hillman had once won a bet that he could keep goal in a charity match with one hand tied behind his back and not concede a goal. At Stoke, on that farcical goalless afternoon, he had no need to handle the ball at all. Indeed, he had already bet someone that he would not concede four goals in Burnley's four test matches. He had let in three before the Stoke stroll and there was no chance of a fourth going past him that afternoon.

The Stoke–Burnley game goes down in history on two counts. The authority's disgust at the players' actions led to the curtailing of test matches in favour of automatic promotion and relegation, and, secondly, as far as I am aware, it is the only game without a shot at goal played at the highest levels. There have been games where teams have settled for a result by mutual consent, notably West Germany's 1–0 win over Austria, which enabled both countries to progress to the next group of the 1982 World Cup Finals, and the relegation-escaping 2–2 draw between Coventry and Bristol City in 1977; and there have always been goalless games which tested spectators' patience. When Chelsea met Portsmouth in an end-of-season goalless bore in 1932, the highlight of the game was when the ball burst. 'The ball's packed up,' shouted one spectator. 'Why don't you do the same?'

Any survivors from the Stoke-Burnley pantomime would have sympathised.

COMPLETED –
15 WEEKS LATER

SHEFFIELD, NOVEMBER 1898,
MARCH 1899

At half-time on a drab November Saturday, Argus-Jud, a Birmingham press-man, bet a Sheffield reporter a cigar and a cognac that the game wouldn't be completed. He won his bet – the game was abandoned ten minutes from time – but the Sheffield man might have felt he had cause for a refund when he heard the Football League's decision. In the 1890s each abandoned game was treated on its merits rather than automatically replayed. For some, the score was allowed to stand. For others, as in the case of this Sheffield Wednesday–Aston Villa game, the game had to be completed at a later date. The problems started when the match referee, Aaron Scragg, a Crewe fuel agent and FA Councillor, missed his Manchester train connection by ten seconds. He telegraphed to the Sheffield Wednesday offices, but these were some distance from Wednesday's ground. By kick-off time (2.30p.m.) no one knew where the referee was.

The game started seven minutes late. A local Football League referee, Fred Bye, took charge until Aaron Scragg arrived at half-time. About 17,000 were present, a good-sized crowd considering Wednesday were on the slide and the weather was dire. It had rained all morning and a keen, piercing wind blew towards the Heeley end. The ground was heavy and the ball fell dead at times. It was also very, very gloomy.

Wednesday took the lead after 20 minutes, Crawshaw's shot hitting the legs of three or four defenders and zigzagging into the net. Aston Villa equalised a minute later. Frank Bedingfield, a late replacement at centre-forward, hooked Smith's centre into the net. It was the only Football League goal Bedingfield would ever score. Three years later he collapsed after playing an FA Cup tie for Portsmouth and he died of consumption in South Africa not long afterwards.

A goal by Dryburgh gave Wednesday a 2–1 half-time lead. The next goal – Hemmingfield's header giving Wednesday a 3–1 lead – was awarded by match-referee Aaron Scragg, who had finally found his way to the ground. But Scragg's difficulties continued. The pitch was in semi-darkness. Players tried to spot the white shorts or striped shirts that weren't too muddy. Spectators listened for the sounds of players shouting. Some could see the ball only when it was punted above the level of the stands.

There were just over ten minutes left to play when protests by Devey of Aston Villa led to Aaron Scragg consulting a linesman. The game was abandoned and the debate began. Wednesday claimed that their 3–1 lead was the springboard for almost certain victory and they should be awarded the game. Reporters agreed that, from what they could see, Villa looked very unlikely to recover. On the other hand, Villa claimed Wednesday were to blame for arranging such a late kick-off; they should have known November days were gloomy, and therefore the whole match should be replayed.

The Football League, in their wisdom, compromised. They decided the extra ten-and-a-bit minutes should be played on a convenient date. So the game continued … 15 weeks later.

One conundrum was how to start the game. Would Aaron Scragg remember where the ball was when he abandoned the game, so that he could drop it from the right place?

A second conundrum was the eligibility of players. Would the same 22 men be forced to resume their places?

A third problem was the likely low attendance. Who would turn out to watch the last ten minutes of a game when the result was cut-and-dried?

The Football League ruled that play would start in the usual manner – tossing a coin for choice of ends and then a place-kick – and that any registered player could take part. In the event, Villa used 13 players and Wednesday 16. No doubt the club secretary needed an abacus to decide how the win bonus would be divided.

Someone had a bright idea to entice the crowd. After the ten-minute farce, the two teams would play a 90-minute friendly (light permitting). The proceeds of the friendly would go to Wednesday's Harry Davis, whose benefit match a few weeks before was very badly attended. (On this occasion 3,000 people turned up and Wednesday beat Villa 2–0.)

For 15 weeks Wednesday had desperately needed the two points held in abeyance. Relegation was probable, whereas Villa were favourites for the League Championship. During the infamous 630 seconds of the replay, Wednesday added a further goal to make it a 4–1 victory, but it didn't keep them in the First Division. Villa won the Championship.

This was not the only Football League game to be completed at a later date – Stoke were once ordered to Wolverhampton to play five minutes, and Walsall and Newton Heath completed on a second day – but it proved to be the last. Such was the adverse publicity that the Football League changed its rules over abandoned matches.

More recently there have been at least two similar events in Spain. A 1989 match between Osasuna and Real Madrid was abandoned after 43 minutes, and the remaining 47 minutes were played just before the end of the season. Osasuna led 1–0 after 43 minutes but Hugo Sanchez equalised three months later. In the second, the 1995 Spanish Cup final between Deportivo La Coruna and Valencia, the first attempt was abandoned after 79 minutes, so the two teams returned two days later and played the remaining 11 minutes.

THE PENALTY-KICKING ELEPHANT

LEICESTER, LATE 1890s

Sanger's Circus was in town. They had an elephant who was unbeaten in penalty-kick competitions. When the circus proprietor issued a challenge to Leicester Fosse professional footballers – no one can beat our elephant – it was a challenge too good to miss. Four Leicester Fosse players accepted and took on the elephant.

For each competition the player and the elephant would take four penalties each. The ball, it must be said, favoured the elephant. It was about six times the size of a normal football.

Three of the four Fosse players lost to the elephant. The last hope was William Keech, who used a crafty penalty-taking technique. Keech feinted to play the ball one side of the elephant, then, as the elephant raised its foot in anticipation, Keech slotted the ball into the other corner. The elephant had met a worthy opponent, but hung on to draw 2–2. A replay was ordered. This time Keech's deceptions were too much for the elephant, who went under 3–2.

So, if you ever get around to picking a team from the animal kingdom to play one of those world teams selected in the back of a football autobiography, please don't forget about the elephant. He may not have much mobility but, with a spot of training, could warrant a place on the substitutes' bench, just in case the game should go to a penalty shoot-out.

A TEMPESTUOUS
SEMI-FINAL

NOTTINGHAM, BOLTON, MANCHESTER
AND DERBY, MARCH 1899

Willie Foulke, goalkeeper for England and Sheffield United (and later Chelsea), was probably the largest footballer ever. He started his career at 15st (95.2kg) and ended it at 22st (138kg). Well over 6ft (1.8m) tall, he dwarfed players and became a legend with his variable moods.

Talk about strength. Foulke could easily carry a man under each arm. He could punch a football to the halfway-line. And talk about girth. The ground rumbled and the stadium darkened when he came out to narrow the angle, an exceedingly difficult man to put the ball past. He was big enough to save penalties without doing too much, as, in his day, goalkeepers were allowed to advance when penalty-kicks were being taken.

Willie Foulke was also legendary at giving away penalties. On one occasion he picked up a forward around the waist and threw him into the net to concede a penalty. Another time, during a League game in the 1898–9 season, he picked up Liverpool centre-forward George Allan, turned him upside-down and stood him on his head in the mud. The resultant penalty turned the game Liverpool's way.

Imagine, then, the effect of the semi-final draw later that same season: Liverpool against Sheffield United. George Allan against Willie Foulke.

Foulke was in great form that year. On one occasion he kept Sheffield United in the FA Cup competition with a brilliant save but tore a thigh muscle in the process. The stretchers weren't big enough to carry him off. It needed six men instead. He was fit enough for the semi-final. The first attempt was at Nottingham. Hedley gave Sheffield United the lead. The equaliser, from Foulke's old adversary Allan, was inevitably greeted with a surly glare. Morgan gave Liverpool a half-time lead. Sheffield United rescued a 2–2 draw with a goal from Walter 'Cocky' Bennett.

The next attempt to settle the tie, at Bolton, had twice as many goals. Twice Liverpool were two goals ahead (2–0 and 4–2) but two goals in the last eight minutes by Priest saved Sheffield United. Allan again scored one of the Liverpool goals.

The third game was at Fallowfield. The crowd invaded the pitch and played their own game. During the 90-minute first half – half the time spent clearing the pitch – Allan gave Liverpool the lead and there was the much-anticipated clash between Foulke and the goalscorer. The Liverpool centre-forward, a hotheaded Scottish international, was nothing but a nuisance to the Sheffield United goalkeeper.

Foulke had the last laugh of that semi-final. The Fallowfield game was abandoned at half-time, and Sheffield United won the fourth attempt, 1–0 at Derby. The Cup Final, by comparison to the semi-final, was an afternoon out. Sheffield United won the trophy by beating Derby County 4–1.

Altogether Willie Foulke played in three FA Cup Finals for Sheffield United, winning two and losing one. After the game at Crystal Palace in 1902, Foulke was incensed at the decision to allow Southampton's goal, scored late in the game by Harry Wood. Lying in the bath, contemplating the replay, his temper snapped with typical idiosyncrasy. He stormed out of the dressing-area and stalked the Crystal Palace corridors in search of the referee and linesmen, 20st (127kg) of steaming nudity. It must have been one of the strangest sights of the century.

SOCCER SICKNESS
LIVERPOOL, JANUARY 1902

The Stoke City management made a serious tactical error before the game at Liverpool – they allowed all the players to eat plaice for lunch. After the half-time interval in the game, only seven Stoke players were fit to resume. The Stoke secretary, Mr Austerberry, was very sympathetic. He was as sick as any of them.

Stoke goalkeeper Dick Roose was in distress before the game started. Roose, a Welsh international, was known as an adventurous goalkeeper whose tactics of wandering all over the field were not curbed until the 1912 change of law. On this day Roose could think only of wandering off the field … as quickly as possible. He lasted just ten minutes, by which time Stoke were a goal behind.

'Who wants to go in goal, lads? Come on, someone will have to go in.'

Meredith was the unlucky Stoke player appointed as deputy goalkeeper. For the rest of the first half, during which time he conceded three goals, Meredith made frantic gestures to indicate he would be happier out of goal. His captain, Johnstone, merely flashed back encouraging smiles.

At half-time the busiest man in the dressing-room was Dr Moody, a Stoke director, who examined most of the players and detected signs of lead poisoning. Moody had made his own way to the ground and had therefore escaped the midday meal.

Roose and Ashworth were the most afflicted of the Stoke players, and it was apparent that they would take no further part in the match. Dr Moody also recommended that Watkins and Whitehouse remain in the dressing-room. The only two people in the Stoke party seemingly unaffected were the two trainers, who had passed over the fish at lunch-time.

Dr Moody was left in no doubt about the seriousness of the illnesses. He said later: 'In fact the dressing-room resembled the cabin of a cross-Channel steamer in bad weather, and smelt like it ... only more so.'

Stoke started the second half with seven players. They played with a goalkeeper – still Meredith – one back, two halves and three forwards. And did quite well too. There was a short spell when Liverpool failed to score.

While people were beginning to debate at what point the game might be abandoned, the two missing forwards, Watkins and Whitehouse, gallantly reappeared against doctor's orders. Goalkeeper Roose, meanwhile, who had a pulse-rate of 148 per minute when he left the field, would need a few hours' rest to recover.

In his absence Liverpool scored some soft goals. Not until the sixth went in did Meredith have his wish granted; Clarke took over in goal.

The final total was seven. Not Stoke's favourite number. They had seven fit men, conceded seven goals ... and lost the next seven games.

FISHERMEN VS FIREMEN
SCARBOROUGH, DECEMBER 1905

The game between the fishermen and engineer deck-hands of Scarborough and district steam trawlers was an annual fixture on Boxing Day during the 1900s.

The venue was Scarborough's South Sands. Goalposts were sunk in barrels, top hats were worn, and a procession of decorated tramcars paraded through the main streets on the morning of the match. The Rifle Volunteer Band played as the firemen and fishermen played football. In 1905, the fishermen won 5–3, but the firemen made amends by winning the tug-of-war competition held afterwards.

The 1905 game was particularly important because the remarkably fine weather helped produce record receipts. The proceeds of the game were handed over to two widows. The deceased men were John Lancaster, a well-known Scarborough cobleman, and Robert Thompson, who had been prominent in local footballing circles.

This unusually large gathering of trawlermen also provided the opportunity for other business. Burton Truefitt, a fisherman on a Hartlepool trawler, was presented with a gold watch to commemorate an occasion when he attempted to rescue a colleague at sea.

The gold watch contained the following inscription: 'Presented to Burton Truefitt for his heroic attempt to save the life of the late George Whittleton who was drowned at sea, September 23rd 1905, from the steam trawler St Mary.'

UNDER THE SCORCHING SUN

MANCHESTER, SEPTEMBER 1906

At half-time Manchester City players could talk only of the sun, those who could still talk. Outside it was more than 90°F (32°C) in the shade – too hot for sunbathing. There had been no forewarning of the unbearable heat for the newcomers to the City team, especially the Scottish imports, and it was virtually a new-look team because 17 City players and ex-players had recently been suspended by the FA. On the first day of the season, City were sunshocked and shellshocked.

Harry Newbould was the new secretary-manager of Manchester City – several officials had also been suspended after the FA inquiry into financial affairs – and he must have been desolate when he saw the dressing-room scene at half-time. City were 2–0 down to Woolwich Arsenal, three players looked incapable of continuing and it was 60 years before the use of substitutes. Thornley and Grieve were flat on their backs, too ill with sunstroke to do any more work that day. Little Jimmy Conlin, who had sensibly taken the field with a handkerchief tied over his head, had been forced to take refuge in the dressing-room a few minutes before half-time. City were down to eight men.

In Harry Newbould's day, managers were not the strategic conjurors and media magic-men that they are today. Their role was mainly to sign players, pin up team-sheets and ensure the players were all in the right railway carriage.

Newbould was one of the more enterprising of his ilk, and at half-time he might have had some say about tactics on that scorching day. Translated into more modern managerial hype, the message conveyed to the City players would have been something like this: 'Right, lads, I know it was a bad toss to lose, and it's not the best of conditions, but we'll have the sun on our backs this second half and it'll be the same for them. It's only 11 of them against eight of us. No, Bill, it won't be like this every week in Manchester. Okay, lads, we're two down, and we've only got eight men, but we can go out and take the game to them. I want us to play a 1–3–3 formation this half. That's one full-back, three half-backs and three forwards. And we'll try to catch them offside. Yes, I know you don't know each other very well and only a couple of you have played for City before, but look at it this way, it'll be easier to get to know seven others than ten others. This is a great chance for a good start to the season. And, remember, if you hear the crowd cheering, they're cheering for you, not because they've seen the sun in Manchester.'

Whatever Newbould or anybody else actually said at half-time, it certainly did the trick. Even though City had lost three forwards with sunstroke, they pushed a defender into the forward-line and played a 1–3–3 formation. In the fiftieth minute Jimmy Conlin returned to the field and the crowd cheered as if they'd seen the sun for the first time.

Taking his position in what was now a 1–3–4 formation, Conlin made a goal for Dorsett, and City, only 2–1 down, were back in the game. But that was as far as it went. Dorsett collapsed soon afterwards, the heat struck down Kelso and Buchan, and City were down to five fit men plus the plucky Conlin.

The referee spoke to his linesmen, but they agreed that there was no just cause for abandoning the game. The Woolwich Arsenal players, meanwhile, were far less affected. They scored two more goals, taking the score to

4–1, but sportingly didn't cash in too much when they faced five fit men in the closing stages of the game.

It took City some time to recover from this setback – two days later they lost 9–1 at Everton – but the new-look team pulled together sufficiently to keep the club in the First Division.

THE CIRCUS GAME

BIRKENHEAD, AUTUMN 1910

There is a particular breed of professional footballer who frowns on people tinkering with the rules of the game. Circus acts belong in the circus, he may say when he discovers a lighthearted experiment at a village fête or local sports. A team once entered a five-a-side competition wearing gorilla suits. Unfortunately one player collapsed with breathing difficulties.

One excellent example of the 'circus game' was that at a village sports near Birkenhead in 1910. A match was arranged between two teams with different handicaps. One team had their arms tied to their sides and their boots and stockings removed. The players of the other team were mounted on stilts, 6ft (1.8m) high.

A report in *Thomson's Weekly News* summarised the play: 'The contest was not so unequal as might have been expected for though those on stilts found it difficult to touch the ball, their antagonists discovered how important a part the arms play in maintaining balance, and when they attempted to run they fell in all directions. In the end the tied arm team won.'

Personally I am not convinced. I am sure I would rather play in a tied arm team than on 6ft stilts, and I wouldn't want to be responsible for anybody who tried to prove me wrong.

THE 'TONYPANDEMONIUM' GAME

TONYPANDY, NOVEMBER 1910

They called it 'Tonypandemonium' when striking South Wales coal-miners rioted and Home Secretary Winston Churchill sent in troops, but the civil unrest had barely died down when the soldiers played the strikers at football.

On Monday 31 October about 12,000 Tonypandy coal-miners downed tools. The four pits involved were members of the Cambrian combine. A week later pickets answered a bugle call at 4a.m. and took to the streets in force. They posted themselves at every street corner and at the entrances to each of the four Cambrian collieries.

The pickets' violence against the collieries included raking fires from the boilers and stoning the buildings, but that was small-scale compared with the events of Tuesday evening. Shop windows were smashed and the contents were looted.

Troops were called in. A detachment of the North Lancashire Regiment arrived on the Wednesday evening. Less than a week later Major-General Macready reported that order was restored. His report contained a small reference to the evidence of normality: 'A football match between the strikers and the soldiers was played at Tonypandy in which the soldiers were victorious.' Winston Churchill replied, 'Pray consult me on any points which cause you embarrassment,'.

The match took place on 15 November at the mid-Rhondda ground. The Lancashire Fusiliers, by far the better team, beat mid-Rhondda Athletic 4–1. Each goal was cheered heartily.

THE ELECTION CAMPAIGN GAME

MIDDLESBROUGH, DECEMBER 1910

Middlesbrough's home match with top-of-the-table Sunderland was scheduled for two days before the 1910 General Election. Middlesbrough chairman Colonel F. Gibson Poole, twice mayor of Middlesbrough, was standing as Unionist candidate for the local constituency. The incumbent Member of Parliament, Penry Williams, a Liberal, was favourite to be returned. Colonel Gibson Poole needed all the extra support he could muster. A good win against neighbours Sunderland might swing a few votes.

The key incident, as revealed to an FA Commission later, took place before the match. It was alleged that Middlesbrough's secretary-manager, Andy Walker, approached Charlie Thomson, Sunderland's Scottish international captain, offering £30 – £10 for Thomson, £2 for each of his team-mates – and saying it was for the colonel's sake, as it would make a big difference to Monday's election. The news of this approach soon spread through Sunderland's ranks – from captain to trainer to a director to the chairman, who reported it to the Football Association. An FA Commission later agreed that an illegal approach had been made. Colonel Gibson Poole and Andy Walker were suspended permanently. A separate FA Commission investigated the Middlesbrough club in more detail and found 'distinct and flagrant tampering with the books' that same season.

There are two results to announce. On the Saturday, Middlesbrough won by a single goal, scored in the first half when they had the wind behind them. In the second half, they hung on and defended desperately.

On the Monday, Colonel Gibson Poole went down by 3,745 votes, a slightly increased majority for Penry Williams, mainly because there was no Labour candidate at this election. Or perhaps the 1–0 victory just wasn't enough.

I have no details on the voting, but Nicholl scored the goal.

DEATH OF A REFEREE
WATTSTOWN, MARCH 1912

The valleys of South Wales have never been an easy territory for soccer referees – heavy, muddy grounds, intense rivalry, fervent supporters and players who usually had their origins in a rugged coal-mining environment. The old chestnut about what's in the game for referees – a small match fee, expenses and a decent funeral – turns sour when we consider the case of William Ernest Williams of Porth, near Pontypridd.

On 15 March 1912 Williams refereed a game at Wattstown, where Aberaman Athletic were the visitors. After the game Williams was brutally attacked while washing himself in the dressing-room. He died as a result of his injuries.

The player responsible, Hansford of Wattstown, was arrested and remanded for trial. He was sentenced to a month's imprisonment for manslaughter.

Several months later, Williams's mother attempted to recover £200 from the South Wales and Monmouthshire FA in an action under the Workmen's Compensation Act. The case, heard at Pontypridd County Court (January 1913), ruled that the referee's contract with the Association was not a contract of service and, anyway, he was paid by the clubs, not the Association. Had the referee been killed during the game, however, it might have been a different story.

BATTLE AT HALF-TIME
BELFAST, SEPTEMBER 1912

Revolvers and knives, sticks and stones, fists and feet. All were used in the battle at Celtic Park. At half-time the Belfast Celtic pitch was a seething mass of struggling men, the police unable to cope.

The riot started suddenly, but many people suspected that it was premeditated. Celtic Park was a Roman Catholic preserve. Linfield, Belfast Celtic's opponents that day, was another Belfast club but with a Protestant following.

Once on the pitch, the crowd split into two factions, one carrying a Union Jack, the other displaying the Belfast Celtic colours of green and white. Thousands were involved in the riot, and the police were swept away in the battle. The din was deafening.

For a time it appeared that people would be killed, but everyone survived the day. The nearby hospital worked over-time to deal with the 100 people who were injured, treating gunshot wounds, fractured skulls and facial injuries.

Hardly anyone was neutral, but if we had to trust a judgement we might rely on the match referee more than others. Mr J.H. Holmes told his story to the newspaper: 'Everything went right to the interval, when, before we could realise it, the pandemonium broke out. We were in the dressing-room at the time, and the officials and players were virtually prisoners. Even when the police reinforcements arrived we were unable to leave, although no attempt was made to molest the club officials or myself. We had a rough time, however, as the departing rioters made a fierce attack on the dressing-room, absolutely wrecking it. The gate money was in an inner room, and even this for a time was in jeopardy, the officials pushing a drawer which contained it against the door as a barricade, which fortunately held good until the rioters passed. During the hottest part of the siege the officials crouched behind, expecting every moment to be struck by stones or overwhelmed by the crowd. We had four policemen laid out in a room at once.'

The riot raged for more than half an hour. There was no hope of restarting the game, which was abandoned at half-time with Linfield leading by a single goal, scored neatly by Smith from McEwen's centre after half an hour's play. It was the only neat thing that happened at Belfast's Celtic Park that afternoon.

THE TEAM AWARDED FOUR PENALTIES

BURNLEY, FEBRUARY 1913

It is hard to imagine that the FA Cup competition passed through the first 20 years of its existence without the concept of the penalty-kick. Then, in a quarter-final game at Trent Bridge in 1891, Notts County's Hendry fisted out a shot that was obviously going through the goal. Opponents Stoke lost 1–0 because the laws had no just punishment for such an offence. Penalty-kicks, along the lines of those recently introduced in Ireland, were suggested.

Amateurs objected, arguing that the presence of a penalty-kick law implied a slur upon their moral behaviour on the field and might even encourage unsportsmanlike behaviour. For many years amateur players refused to recognise the penalty-kick law. If the Corinthians conceded a penalty their goalkeeper would stand by a goalpost until it had been taken.

When the penalty-kick was first introduced, goalkeepers were permitted to advance 6 yards (5.5m) from their goal-line. Some were especially quick off the mark and looked likely to reach the ball before the penalty-taker. In the early 1900s players began to counter by lifting the ball over the head of the advancing goalkeeper. Since 1905 a new law has restricted goalkeepers from moving from the goal-line. (Two more amendments were adopted in the 1920s – one to stop goalkeepers moving their feet, after a trend of off-putting ape-like gestures from keepers, and one to introduce the

10-yard arc to stop teams lining a ten-man phalanx along the edge of the penalty area and thus restricting the taker's run-up to 6 yards/5.5m.)

These were the circumstances, therefore, when Scott of Grimsby Town faced up to four Burnley penalty-kicks on 13 February 1909. The game was played on a very heavy ground and Grimsby suffered two early setbacks. First, Abbott put Burnley ahead. Next, Grimsby lost the injured Lee and had to play the last 70 minutes with ten men.

At first Grimsby played the one-back formation, the old-time equivalent of a sweeper. This was tantamount to setting an offside trap – in those days three defenders rather than two had to be behind the attacker – and made things difficult for Burnley. Even so, Scott broke free and was tripped by Henderson – the first penalty. Scott made a fine save.

Next Wheelhouse handled – the second penalty. Smith took the kick and again Scott moved quickly to make a good save. The Grimsby goalkeeper also saved the follow-up shot but in the resultant scramble somebody handled – the third penalty. Up stepped Abbott, who relieved Burnley supporters by giving his team a 2–0 half-time lead. Two out of three penalties saved, one scored.

After half-time Grimsby abandoned their one-back game in favour of a more orthodox defence and four forwards. They were reduced to nine players when Whitehouse left the field for 'repairs to his knickers' and while he was absent Davidson fouled Abbott – the fourth penalty.

Goalkeeper Scott was still on a hat-trick of penalty saves. Abbott made it easy for him. He shot straight at the goalkeeper. Scott's three penalty saves was a remarkable performance. In the last two months the goalkeeper had saved seven of eight penalties he had faced. Grimsby supporters feared that the defence might recklessly concede penalties, secure in the knowledge that Scott would save them – a mistaken belief, as it proved.

THE WAR GAME
NO MAN'S LAND, DECEMBER 1914

The trench warfare of the First World War was bloody and slaughterous. British and German soldiers climbed from their respective trenches and charged at each other with murderous abandon. British troops would go over the top with a battle-cry, singing, or, in the case of the East Surrey Regiment on at least one occasion, kicking a football.

Deep down, however, many soldiers knew they were fighting a politicians' war. At times the soldiers at the front had sympathy for each other. From the safety of their trenches they might hold shouted conversations, words travelling across No Man's Land, some of the Germans understanding and speaking English. The conversation could easily turn to football – some Germans had been in England before the war – and the most natural thing for men to do was to challenge each other to a game.

There might have been more contests had footballs always been available. The game most frequently mentioned was that on Christmas Day 1914, when British and German soldiers met in No Man's Land to play their international match. The next day they were fighting again.

ONE-ARMED MEN VS WOMEN

READING, SEPTEMBER 1917

Here was a game strange on four counts. Women played against men; the opposing teams were English and Canadian; the men played with hands behind their backs; and the final score was 8–5.

Perhaps the oddest thing was that men were allowed to play against the women on a Southern League ground. After an early wave of women's soccer in the late 1890s, inspired by the Rational Dress movement and generally believed to be organised by Nettie Honeyball in England and Lady Florence Dixie in Scotland, the FA Council (on 25 August 1902) issued instructions not to permit matches against 'lady teams'. They had a policy of separation – men against men, women against women.

That didn't stop women copying men. In the mid-1900s, six-a-side soccer on roller-skates was introduced for men at Brighton skating-rink, and women soon took up the sport. The goals – 6ft (1.8m) high and 7ft (2.1m) wide – were larger than ice-hockey goals, and a regulation-size football containing a pint of water (to keep it from rising) was used. Players were allowed two minutes for skate-repair.

During the First World War, with men away in the forces and women adopting male roles, there was a boom in women's soccer. Although the most lasting development of this period was the Dick-Kerr's factory team in Preston, there were outbreaks all over the country, usually based around factories.

The standard picked up enormously. Back in 1895, 'Lady Correspondent' of the *Manchester Guardian* had been gently scathing about how well the North and South players knocked the ball about: 'They danced around the ball when they reached it as if uncertain what to do with it, much after the manner of a lapdog which has accidentally laid hold of the cat which he has made an elaborate show of pursuing.' But by the end of the First World War the women could play a bit. The Portsmouth *Football Mail* claimed that Pioneer Ladies captain Ada Anscombe was 'the finest woman player in the country', and alleged that a male team once offered two of their men for her. The FA wouldn't have approved.

The wartime games were usually for charity, and the ladies who played a team of convalescing Canadian soldiers at Elm Park in September 1917 had already handed over £161 to various charities that year. Unfortunately, on this Wednesday afternoon, the conditions were vile. The receipts were probably swallowed up by expenses.

After a band from Bearwood Hospital had played, Surgeon-General Foster, director of the Canadian Medical Services, kicked off. The referee was Colonel Mayus, director of bayonet fighting and physical training. No decisions were disputed.

The women won 8–5 with goals from Miss Barrell (3), Miss Small (2), Miss Wragg (2) and Miss Bentley. It was suspected that the Canadian soldiers were too gallant to win, and in any event there must have been great amusement at the sight of them playing with hands behind their backs. Whether this rule was introduced to balance the sides or to make the women feel safer, I do not know.

SOCCER IN GAS MASKS
VARIOUS LOCATIONS, 1917–18

The Royal Engineers have a rich soccer heritage, so it isn't surprising to discover their participation in gas-mask soccer during the First World War.

During the first seven years of the FA Cup (1871–8), the Royal Engineers faced 32 Cup ties, winning the trophy once and reaching the FA Cup Final on three other occasions. They appeared in the first-ever FA Cup Final (1872) and might have done better than a 1–0 defeat had full-back Lieutenant Cresswell not broken his collarbone after ten minutes.

A Royal Engineers team also won the FA Amateur Cup in 1908, and memories of this success were very clear when the First World War broke out. The gas-mask games became a regular part of their training towards the end of the war.

When the whistle went for the kick-off, each player had to take out his gas mask and fit it properly. He wasn't allowed to touch the ball until his mask was properly secured.

During the game the referee would stop the game by whistle and order gas masks to be removed. This time the masks had to be properly put away before players were allowed to touch the ball. The aim, of course, was to familiarise the Royal Engineers with the dexterity needed to use gas masks. The players wore full army uniform during these games, and officers hoped for no serious injuries.

If the notion of soldiers sustaining injuries in soccer games rather than war combat sounds ironic, consider the case of Eddie Mason, a member of the Dragoon Guards for seven years. Mason fought at Marne, Ypres and Aisne and survived the bloodiest war in history with hardly a scratch. Then, in 1919, playing his first game for Hull City, he was carried off in the first few minutes and missed the whole season.

WILFRED MINTER'S GOALSCORING FEAT

DULWICH, NOVEMBER 1922

Never has one man made such a strange goal-scoring impact on a game than Wilfred Minter did that dark Wednesday afternoon in Dulwich. The occasion was an FA Cup replay in the fourth round of the qualifying stage of the competition. In the original game, the previous Saturday, St Albans City and Dulwich Hamlet had drawn 1–1 in controversial circumstances. There was major debate as to whether Redvers Miller's corner-kick had touched any other player before it entered the net – not until 1924 were goals direct from corner-kicks permitted – but referee Rolfe decided it had and St Albans had their late equaliser.

Wilf Minter had been St Albans' outstanding forward in the first game between these two teams of amateurs. He was a local lad, having attended the Hatfield Road school and received football tuition from J. Dickinson, a former St Albans City captain. Minter entered the army when war broke out. While serving overseas he developed his fitness and football talents, and, after demobilisation, played for his school old boys' team, helping them to win the 1919–20 Aubrey Cup competition. He joined St Albans City in February 1921 and soon became a goal-scoring phenomenon for club and county. Representative honours followed, but he turned down professional offers to enter his father's business and remain as an amateur with St Albans.

He was to create a record which no professional has ever matched.

The game was played at Champion Hill, Dulwich, where both the home team and St Albans were forced to field deputy goalkeepers after injuries on the Saturday. No doubt this contributed to the afternoon's entertainment. Alf Fearn, a half-back from St Albans Gasworks, was never likely to be a genius at handling corner-kicks and crosses.

Inside 15 minutes Dulwich were a goal ahead. Then Wilf Minter took over. He scored from a crossbar rebound, headed in a Pierce centre and added a third after exchanging passes with H.S. Miller.

After half an hour the score was clear-cut: Dulwich 1 (Kail), St Albans 3 (Minter 3).

During the next half-hour Alf Fearn's lack of goalkeeping experience was exposed. Dulwich scored four times.

After 60 minutes, therefore, the score conveyed a different message: Dulwich Hamlet 5 (Davis 3, Kail 2), St Albans City 3 (Minter 3).

All over? Not quite. When Harold Figg's shot hit a goalpost, Minter followed up to pull back a goal, then he shot two more to give St Albans the lead.

Seventy minutes played, and again the score was transformed: Dulwich Hamlet 5 (Davis 3, Kail 2), St Albans City 6 (Minter 6).

In these earlier days of soccer, people would dispute what was a real hat-trick. To conform with the cricketing model – three wickets in three consecutive balls – soccer goals really needed to be three in a row rather than three in a game. But here there was no dispute. Minter had done it twice in one game – three in a row in 12 first-half minutes and three in a row again in 10 second-half minutes. Astonishing.

And there was more to come. Five minutes from the end Dulwich put the ball in the St Albans net. The referee reversed his original decision and gave a goal, much to the dismay of the St Albans players. It meant the scores were level at 6–6 after 90 minutes. Extra-time of 15 minutes each way began in fading light.

After 100 minutes Kail sprinted from the halfway-line and gave Dulwich Hamlet a 7–6 lead. In the gathering gloom, at the other end, Minter was tackled clumsily in the penalty area. Appeals for a penalty were turned down. Too dark for the referee to see, some argued.

With just four minutes to play Redvers Miller took a corner-kick for St Albans City. This time there was no doubt that someone touched the ball before it hit the net – Wilfred Minter.

Imagine the mood of the man now. Seven goals each and he has scored all his team's goals. The referee is set to blow his whistle as the 120 minutes are just about played. Then the linesman flags and the referee awards a dubious free-kick to Dulwich. Over comes the cross, Davis heads a goal for the London side. The game ends.

Dulwich Hamlet 8 (Davis 4, Kail 3, Nicol), St Albans City 7 (Minter 7).

For an individual to score seven goals is not all that uncommon, but to score *all* his team's goals including two hat-tricks, and for the *losing* team – that was unique. The next Saturday Wilfred Minter was made captain and the band played 'For he's a jolly good fellow' when he went to the centre of the field for the coin-tossing ritual.

Whether it would have been better to win 1–0 than lose 8–7, we will leave for the modern-day managers to discuss.

EXPERIMENTING WITH THE RULES

LONDON, JANUARY 1925

The Football Association sensed that the offside law needed a radical overhaul. Ivan Sharpe, writing in *Forty Years in Football*, credits, or perhaps discredits, Morley and Montgomery, Notts County full-backs before the First World War, with the invention of the offside tactic. Bill McCracken, Newcastle United's Irish international full-back, took the idea and developed it further. In McCracken's heyday, the later 1900s and early 1910s, the offside law demanded three players goalside of the attacker. Two full-backs with strategic minds, like McCracken and Frank Hudspeth, would combine to catch out players. As McCracken described it much later, it was putting players offside rather than waiting for them to get offside.

When Newcastle played Notts County the game would be wedged in a 20-yard (18.3m) section in the middle of the pitch with both teams hoping to spring the offside traps. Soon other teams caught on to the defensive tactics. Free-kicks became plentiful, scoring more difficult, and entertainment was not the same. It was generally agreed that something should be done to make the offside law fairer to forwards.

On 25 January 1925, the Football Association took advantage of the fact that several clubs, knocked out of the FA Cup, had a blank Saturday. Several experimental games were organised.

The game at Highbury, a friendly between Arsenal and Chelsea, captured the spirit of the experiments. In the first half a line was drawn 40 yards (36.6m) from each goal, limiting the area in which players could be offside. In the second half the referee enforced a rule reducing the number of defenders needed between the player of the ball and the goal from three to two. There was only one offside decision in the whole game – there was only one goal too (scored by Chelsea) – and referee Mr Todman (from Croydon) found it a pleasure not needing to blow his whistle so much. He preferred the two-man plan to the 40-yard idea. The general conclusion was that the experiment was worth a try in a more competitive setting.

There were several other trial games that day – at Clapton (against Wolves), at Charlton (against Luton), at Norwich (against Cambridge University) and an amateur game between the West Riding and Staffordshire, where the 40-yard line was deemed a success and one observer wondered whether the halfway-line marking was now needed, except for the bit in the centre-circle.

Perhaps the most pertinent comments were those of Mr Pilch, the referee at Norwich, who was quoted in the *Athletic News*: 'If two defenders, instead of three, govern the operation of the offside law, football will be faster and a tremendous amount more interesting. I feel absolutely confident that the suggested alteration will make the game much more interesting for spectators. We must take things as they are, not as we would like them to be.'

After a few more experimental matches during the remainder of the season, the two-man plan was adopted by the Football Association in time for the 1925–6 season.

STRIKERS AGAINST POLICE

PLYMOUTH, MAY 1926

It seems strange that striking trade-unionists would play the police at soccer on the day of their most intense conflict in history, yet such a match occurred in Plymouth during the 1926 General Strike. A crowd of over 10,000 saw the strikers win by two goals to one. The policemen had their work cut out – on and off the field.

Industrial unrest among northern coal-miners had spread to other industries and services. The effects reached Plymouth later than most towns, but the outcome was devastating. At the end of the first week in May the General Strike was a week old, and the *Western Morning News and Mercury* was talking of a state bordering on civil war: 'Football is all very well in normal circumstances, and there is no reason why policemen and workmen should not play it. But conditions today are not normal, and a match between policemen and strikers is, at least, strange.'

The events of the Saturday confirmed some people's worst fears. Tramway employers tempted fate by resuming a modified service using volunteers and inspectors to replace the 800 workers who were on strike. Confrontation and chaos was the result. During the morning crowds gathered in the town-centre to prevent tramcars passing.

By 11.30 that Saturday morning there were around 4,000 people doing their best to block the trams. Amidst the jostling a few stones smashed tramcar windows. About 20 or 30 policemen charged the crowd, wielding batons, but it did not prevent the continued harassment of the tramcars. Ironically, this happened just before the soccer match was due to start at Home Park. Once again the police and the strikers were on opposite sides.

The tramway team scored midway through the first half, and a wave of enthusiasm greeted this first – dare I say it? – strike.

Another ironic touch came at half-time, when the music was provided by the tramway band – workers at the very heart of the dispute. When the second-half started, large sections of the crowd followed the band off the pitch and out of the stadium. By the time the strikers scored their second goal, ten minutes from the end, the tramway band was leading a procession of people, four by four, walking along the tramlines to ensure no cars passed. There were more ugly scenes.

Mounted police were called in to deal with a 20,000 crowd in Old Town Street. Three arrests were made, but the tramcar service was withdrawn and the likelihood of pitched battle averted. The next week the strike was called off, leaving the Plymouth strikers with a 100 per cent record on the soccer pitch. That same month games also took place between the Sheffield Police and strikers at Park Colliery.

AMATEURS VS PROFESSIONALS

MANCHESTER, OCTOBER 1926

Take a team of professionals, familiar with each other's play. Include five England internationals. Then pick a team of assorted amateur players. Now play the amateurs against the professionals. Who would win? Yes, the amateurs, of course. On five occasions, during the 1920s, the Professionals played the Amateurs for the FA Charity Shield. It was soccer's equivalent of the Gentlemen–Players cricket match. There were some who said the professionals played these midweek games with their minds on the week-end Football League programme, but there was certainly pride at stake. In the 1926 Professionals' team there were internationals such as Tom Magee (West Brom), David Jack (Bolton), Bill Rawlings (Southampton), Joe Smith (Bolton) and Fred Tunstall (Sheffield United). The team was selected from the FA party which had toured Canada the previous close-season.

The Professionals scored three goals that afternoon at Maine Road, Manchester, but in between Rawlings's second in the thirtieth minute, and Tunstall's in the last, the Amateurs hit half a dozen. Edgar Kail, a full international before the end of the decade, scored the first. Wilfred Minter scored the second. Macey hit the next two, the second from 25 yards (22.9m), Minter got another, and the sixth was an own-goal. The Amateurs won 6–3.

INTRODUCING THE EIGHT-SQUARE GAME

LONDON, JANUARY 1927

Broadcasting was in its infancy. The idea of putting a soccer match on the BBC and relaying news through the wireless system throughout Britain was original, exciting and challenging. The game chosen for the experiment was Arsenal against Sheffield United, two teams in the middle of Division One. There was nothing special about the game, just that it could capture the attention of people outside Highbury Stadium.

That week the *Radio Times* carried a front-page plan of the Highbury pitch, dividing it into eight equal sections. Each section was numbered for easy identification. Low numbers (one to four) indicated a team's own half of the field, high numbers (five to eight) that it had possession in the opposition half. Odd numbers referred to the left side of the team, even numbers meant the right. The sections were called 'squares', but if they were genuine squares, Highbury must have had a different-shaped pitch that day.

Two commentators were used. Mr Wakelam described the play, and, in the background, Mr Lewis called out the square numbers. This informed the audience who had the ball and exactly where play was occurring. They could sit with the *Radio Times* plan in front of them and follow the verbal action.

This experiment, following closely after the broadcasting of the England–Wales rugby international, was considered a success, though there were some criticisms in newspapers, as might perhaps be expected from a rival reporting network. Some said the account was disconnected, delivered too rapidly or that several players were wrongly identified by the commentators. Well, it was early days.

Appropriately, the first two goals scored on radio, knocked in from squares seven and eight, went to two of the biggest names in soccer at the time – England international Charlie Buchan (Arsenal) and Ireland international Billy Gillespie (Sheffield United). The game finished 1–1.

Soccer broadcasting expanded rapidly. Ten million people, it was estimated, listened to the regular BBC broadcasts of Arsenal director George Allison (commentator) and Derek 'Uncle Mac' McCulloch (square caller), and three months after the Highbury game the FA Cup Final was broadcast. Soccer was on its way to a new era. Local celebrities would become national heroes. Ordinary supporters, accustomed to reading about their team and chatting to one another, would suddenly discover how a player's name sounded with a BBC accent. Blind people would have their interest in soccer resurrected. And commentators learned the power of information.

EIGHT ON A DEBUT
STIRLING, JANUARY 1930

When a strange result occurs, there is usually a set of logical explanations. Take this match, for instance. Why would King's Park, a Scottish Second Division team, beat Forfar Athletic, a team above them in the division, by the ridiculous score of 12–2?

There were four main reasons. First there was the Forthbank pitch, greasy in places, ankle-deep almost everywhere, the sort of clinging, cloying pitch that saps the energy of opponents once a home team gets a substantial lead. Second, there was the Forfar defence, which was missing four regular players. Third, there was the King's Park attack, which included a newcomer called John Dyet, who was on trial at centre-forward. Fourth, there was the date, Thursday 2 January, the day after a full league programme of soccer games, shortly after the celebrations of New Year's Eve.

Perhaps the most dramatic factor was the introduction of Dyet, who replaced Martin, injured in the 3–2 defeat at East Stirling the day before, at centre-forward. Dyet, a Cowie juvenile player, brother of King's Park left-half Gilbert, scored six goals in the first half. At the interval the home team led 7–0, Duffy having scored the third of the seven.

Forfar, who had won 4–3 against Arbroath on New Year's Day, included their own star forward, Davie Kilgour, the Second Division top scorer with 24 goals. Kilgour, likely to be overtaken in two games if Dyet kept up his first-half pace, pulled back a goal with a penalty shortly after half-time.

King's Park added a further three goals, scored by Ross, Baird and Duffy, before Forfar scored again. Then Dyet chipped in with two more goals before the end.

King's Park wasted no time in signing the youngster. Eight goals and a record score seemed as much as could be expected from Dyet on his debut. Besides, there were clubs queuing up outside the Forthbank stadium, just in case he slipped through the net that afternoon.

King's Park ended the season one point above Forfar Athletic in the league table.

EXPOSING CHELSEA'S DEFENCE

BLACKPOOL, OCTOBER 1931

Footballers are soft these days, old-time players are fond of telling us. They play in 'carpet slippers', use balloons as footballs and have games postponed if there's a spot of rain on the pitch. An exaggeration, perhaps, but the old-timers could point to plenty of evidence when Chelsea took a fateful trip to the seaside in October 1931. The game at Blackpool was more a question of how many players would collapse with hypothermia and exposure. At full-time Chelsea were left with six men.

It was a cold, miserable, windy day with ferocious driving rain. Fifteen minutes before kick-off the Bloomfield Road stadium was comparatively deserted. The eventual gathering of 6,000 spectators was about half the usual size. It was a wonder the game started, and Chelsea later complained that the pitch was unfit. Ground staff worked with pitchforks in a futile attempt to clear the water.

Chelsea, missing their famous Scottish International Hughie Gallacher (how glad he must have been), won the toss and sensibly opted to kick with the wind behind them. But conditions soon proved almost impossible. The ball either plopped in mud or squirted over grease. The first chance fell to Jimmy Hampson of Blackpool but he lost the ball in one of the more shallow lakes.

Chelsea found it hopeless to pursue their normal short-passing game and soon trailed to Wilkinson's twelfth-minute goal. Even the referee had difficulty. Mr Jones of Nottingham lost his balance and tumbled to his knees, much to the amusement of the spectators.

In the thirty-first and thirty-fourth minutes Jimmy Hampson scored two freak goals to give Blackpool a 3–0 half-time lead. First the England international centre-forward dribbled round Vic Woodley as the Chelsea goalkeeper lost his footing in the mud. Then Woodley stooped to intercept a cross, fell on both knees, and gasped in amazement as the ball stopped dead in the mud a yard from him. Hampson stepped in, used his foot as a spade and thanked the weather for his second goal.

At half-time came the first sensation. Peter O'Dowd, soon to become England's centre-half, slumped unconscious in the dressing-room. His body temperature had dropped dangerously low. Two other Chelsea players were overcome by the cold. The second half started with only eight in the Chelsea team. Although they were soon restored to ten men, nobody relished the water-polo activities in the Chelsea penalty area. Blackpool's long-ball game was well-suited to the conditions and Hampson completed his hat-trick in the seventy-fifth minute.

Immediately after Blackpool's fourth goal, two Chelsea players left the field. The crowd booed and jeered, but it didn't stop another Chelsea player limping off. Soon there were only six left. And, on the same day (31 October), at nearby Blackburn, two of the home side and three Sheffield United players were treated for exposure, while the referee collapsed from the cold. After a 20-minute delay, a linesman completed the game.

At the end of that season (1931–2), Blackpool escaped relegation from the First Division by one point. They were grateful to the day at Bloomfield Road when Chelsea's defence was exposed to the cold.

But even in the 1930s some old-timers were doubtless arguing that it was tougher in their day. There was a famous occasion at Grimsby (in 1912) when six Leicester Fosse players walked off the pitch ten minutes from the end of their 4–0 defeat, and Leicester trainer Harley Thompson was later suspended for enticing them off. And Ernest Needham, Sheffield United's famous international at the turn of the century, recalled a numbing experience at Aston Villa. Writing in his book *Association Football*, he described it like this: 'The bitterly cold wind and sleet pierced one, numbing muscle and brain. Men on both sides succumbed and were carried away to hot baths and stimulants. I left the field half an hour before the finish of time, and by so doing probably saved my life. Even Foulke was carried in completely exhausted. Several of the Villans did what playing they could in great-coats, and one used an umbrella.'

THE FASTEST
INDIVIDUAL GOALS
WEST HAM, NOVEMBER 1931

Picture yourself as a supporter of a team which hasn't won for four games. (Some will find this easier than others.) Your centre-forward, Richardson, hasn't been playing well. You would prefer Cookson in Richardson's place at centre-forward. Now you have an away game against a team in London, which means a difficult journey of over 100 miles (160km). However, as the London team is not playing well, you think your side has a chance. You decide to go, but have difficulty finding the ground – your team was promoted to the First Division at the end of last season – and arrive late. You make your way on to the terraces and see someone you know.

'How are we doing?' you ask your mate, knowing that you have missed about ten minutes of the game.

'We're four-nil up,' he replies casually. 'Richardson's got all four and he should have had two more.'

Would you believe him?

Yet, that day in November 1931, you would have had to. W.G. Richardson, the West Bromwich Albion centre-forward, had two good chances in the first five minutes and missed them. Then he scored four times in the next five minutes. It was a remarkable spell of sustained rapid goal-scoring, taking advantage of some weak West Ham full-back play and the fact that England international centre-half Jim Barrett was playing out of position at left-half.

The game was virtually over as a contest almost as soon as it had begun. The next goal, scored just after the hour, by Sandford, put West Brom five goals ahead. Jimmy Ruffell headed a reply soon afterwards, and West Ham went down 5–1 on their own ground.

W.G. Richardson's four goals in five minutes is the quickest scoring of four goals on record, a feat equalling that of Jimmy McIntyre of Blackburn Rovers a decade earlier. The difference was that McIntyre's goals came in the second half. Richardson set off one of the quickest starts a soccer game has known.

SIX IN 21 MINUTES

LINCOLN, JANUARY 1932

Lincoln City were at home to Halifax Town. Lincoln had completed more than half of their Division Three North fixtures for the season and only one team had stopped them scoring in a game – Halifax Town. The game at the Shay had finished 3–0 to the home team.

Lincoln, with the wind behind them, scored twice during the first half of the return but play was fairly even. The goals came from Riley and Hall, the latter being in the middle of an exceptionally good run. 'I hav sung of Alan Hall, whos a terrer with the ball,' wrote a rhymer who specialised in the local vernacular.

The goal blitz started in the forty-sixth minute. Lincoln scored seven in 21 minutes, and, strangely, Hall was not among the second-half scorers. Frank Keetley scored six. Wrote our rhymer friend, 'I hay toled of how Frank Keetley, shoots so well and passes needly.'

Keetley, who had missed the previous game due to injury, took advantage of the extra marking on Hall to steer Lincoln to their 9–1 win. Lincoln went to the top of Division Three North and that season they won the championship on goal average. Alan Hall scored 42 League goals – he is still Lincoln's highest scorer in a season – but the home game against Halifax was Frank Keetley's day.

THE GAME WITH TWO REFEREES

CHESTER, JANUARY 1935

Two referees and two linesmen. The idea came from the Referees' Committee. The game chosen for experiment was an England Amateur international trial between teams from the North and South. It was a bad choice. The amateurs were so well-behaved that nothing was tested. One clear-cut penalty was awarded, converted by Simms in the North's 3–1 win, but, otherwise, there were barely enough decisions for one referee, let alone two.

The referees at Chester were Dr A.W. Barton, a Repton schoolmaster from Derby, and Mr E. Wood of Sheffield. Early in the game they were tempted across the halfway line a few times before they realised their more limited responsibilities. Onlookers wondered what would happen if an incident occurred in one referee's half and the other was in a better position to judge. Who would decide then?

A second attempt was made later that season. The same two referees, Barton and Wood, were given control of a professional international trial, England against the Rest. Again the outcome was inconclusive as there was not enough work for two men. The Football Association might have learned more from a competition where the referees were stretched, perhaps at local-league level, rather than the games at Chester and West Bromwich.

Observers' reactions were generally negative. The idea never caught on, the detail was never worked out. The spectators would have needed to distinguish between the two referees (red whistle and yellow whistle?) to know whom to insult. Yet, had the idea been instigated, we might today have players voting in the dressing-rooms and sponsors offering a prize – Referee of the Match.

'AVALANCHE AT ASTON'
ASTON, DECEMBER 1935

Before the away game at bottom-of-the-league Aston Villa, Arsenal centre-forward Ted Drake was worried because he hadn't been scoring too well. He contacted his manager, George Allison, who was in hospital at the time. Allison wrote back indicating how he felt Arsenal could get a 'sackful' of goals against Villa.

On paper it was not an easy fixture. Although Villa were bottom of the First Division, they had spent a lot of money signing new players. Their new team contained six internationals, and it seemed only a matter of time before they put together some good results.

The crowd must have formed the same impression during the first 20 minutes of the game against Arsenal. Villa did most of the attacking but couldn't score. Then Arsenal broke away and Ted Drake scored with his first shot. He also scored with his second, third, fourth, fifth and sixth shots. He hit the cross-bar with his seventh, then slammed in his seventh goal with his eighth attempt of the day. Arsenal won 7–1, Palethorpe scoring for Villa shortly after Drake had notched his second hat-trick.

Drake, in fact, scored a hat-trick in each half. His fifth and sixth goals were struck with the supreme confidence of a man who just could not miss the target. Villa had their chances – Palethorpe nearly made it 1–1 with a header and had the ball in the net at 3–0 only to discover Arsenal had been given a free-kick – but the difference between the teams lay in Drake's finishing.

Ted Drake, a £6,000 signing from Southampton, was still in his early 20s. The next year he scored Arsenal's cup-winning goal at Wembley and he helped them to two League Championships. He won five England caps and, as a manager, took Chelsea to the League Championship in 1954–5. Altogether, it was a remarkable career, although he is remembered by many for that sensational day at Villa Park when he earned headlines, such as 'Drake's Armada' and 'Avalanche at Aston'.

TEN GOALS AT
HIS FIRST ATTEMPT
LUTON, APRIL 1936

Easter Monday at Kenilworth Road. Luton Town, preparing for a Third Division South game against Bristol Rovers, discovered that they had two centre-forwards on the injury list. Manager Ned Liddell opted for Joe Payne as a replacement. Payne, a reserve wing-half, had some experience of playing in the forward-line but not in the Luton first team.

There was no early hint of what was to come. Payne collected a goal in the twenty-third minute and Roberts soon made it 2–0 to Luton, but, five minutes before half-time, the game could have gone either way. Then Joe Payne scored nine in 46 minutes, and no one else scored during this incredible period. With three headers and seven shots, Joe Payne had scored ten goals on his first attempt at centre-forward. Martin scored one in the last minute to make the final score 12–0.

The previous individual scoring record was nine, and Joe Payne's record of ten in a Football League game has held ever since. Payne, a former Derbyshire coal-miner, was 22 years old at the time. Two years later, in 1938, he went to Chelsea for £2,000, already an England international. During the war he twice broke an ankle, and never added to the one cap he won against Finland, when he scored two goals. After the war he scored six League goals for West Ham in a spell of nine months – four goals less than he managed in 63 minutes that sensational day at Luton.

TAKING IT AT
WALKING PACE
DERBY, MAY 1937

This was the sixth annual walking match between the Crewe and Derby Railway Veterans Associations. Derby held the Cup, having won 2–0 at Crewe in 1936, and were looking to win it two years running (not that the referee would have allowed that).

All the players were over 65 years old. The oldest, Young (Derby) and Betley (Crewe), were both 73. The venue was the Baseball Ground, home of Derby County, and 1,500 spectators turned out on a fine day. The game was one of the most bizarre ever refereed by Arthur Kingscott, who had officiated in two FA Cup Finals, but he had no difficulty keeping up with play, which, at times, reached the frenzied pace of 6 miles per hour (9.7km/h).

Crewe started well on top and looked set for a walkaway victory. By comparison Derby looked pedestrian, which, of course, they were. But once Derby discovered their wing men, the pattern of play changed. Their left-wing pair of Collier and Briddon walked rings round the Crewe right flank, while Radford, only 67, put in some good walks and centres on the Derby right. Radford had the best chance of the match, only the goalkeeper to beat, but shot 5 yards (4.6m) wide. The crowd groaned. They felt he could have walked the ball in.

The build-up of both teams was slow, naturally, but there was no holding back by the players. One or two of them received minor knocks but were advised by the trainer to 'walk it off'. There were only two things missing. The occasion deserved a walking commentary from a radio station and it also needed a goal.

The game ended 0–0 and both teams shared the Cup, which was filled to the brim and passed round the players at the end. Crewe were optimistic about their chances the next season, when they would be at home. They had a younger team than Derby – average age 68 as against Derby's 69 – and knew the Derby 'lads' would be a year older when they met again.

A MATTER OF CLASS

ETON, DECEMBER 1938

In December 1938 the playing fields of Eton College staged one of the strangest games of Britain's class-conscious society. The Eton College school team took on St Helen's Auckland Social Service team, which was mainly comprised of unemployed coal-miners from the north-east.

Two years previously, Eton College had 'adopted' the St Helen's Social Club centre as part of a goodwill exercise during the days of severe economic depression. Periodically, the boys and staff of the College had travelled to the Durham village of Auckland, involving themselves in the local community activities. As the *Auckland Chronicle* put it, 'Taking part in the sing-songs, the village teas and suppers, and dances gave them an insight into that quality of warm hospitality which is the quality of the north.'

Now came the opportunity for a trip of a lifetime. The Auckland boys were invited to visit the College at the expense of the Etonians. A game of football was part of the excursion. The tough, gritty northern lads were expected to give the Eton schoolboys a pretty good game.

At 8a.m. on Wednesday 14 December, a party of 18 Auckland boys and seven officials set off by motor-coach on the 250-mile (402-km) journey south. They were cheered loudly by mothers, sisters and sweethearts, who had gathered on a chilly morning to give them a good send-off to the 'far distant land'.

Only six of the party travelling south were in employment. The rest were wondering where their next wage would come from. But for one day the young men from the north-east were given the chance to live like the 1,160 boys at Eton College. On arrival, they were given a hot supper and hotel accommodation. 'They are champion,' one north-easterner said of his southern hosts. 'It's like home from home.'

In the morning the north-east party breakfasted with the schoolboys and attended the Chapel service. Later, after watching work begin in the classrooms, they were taken to see Windsor Castle and St George's Chapel. Then they toured the College buildings and were shown the Tuck Shop – a strategic move, as the football game started shortly afterwards.

The Auckland lads were surprised by the quality of the Eton schoolboys' play. The contest between the polished students and the rough-and-ready unemployed coal-miners was an even one. The result was a 2–2 draw.

The boys ate tea in the College Hall and stayed a second night before travelling home the next day. They agreed that the trip had been grand. One of them, centre-half Makinson, spoke of the best three days of his life.

FREAKISH AND GOALFUL
LIVERPOOL, APRIL 1941

'The most freakish, goalful representative match of all time,' wrote L.E.E. of the *Liverpool Daily Post.* 'It will become one of the talked-of "classics" even if, on this occasion, there was no rabid club partisanship to fire enthusiasms.'

In one respect the reporter was correct – it was the most amazing representative match of all time. In another respect he was sadly wrong – the game between the Football League and a British XI, in aid of the Lord Mayor's Fund, hasn't been mentioned much since that day in April 1941.

Freakishness was quite common during wartime games. Teams were often selected at the last minute because players' availability was in doubt. There are countless examples of double-figure scores being registered against variegated teams containing something like half a dozen assorted professionals, a couple of out-of-position reserves, a cocky local just out of the pub, a spectator who falsely claimed to have played for Aldershot and a trainer playing his first game since Wembley was built.

But this game wasn't like that. The players were all stars. More than half were internationals, nine had played in FA Cup Finals, and there wasn't a laggard amongst them, although there were several decidedly strange incidents.

One of these was the injury of Alf Hobson, the Chester and ex-Liverpool goalkeeper, shortly before half-time. Playing for the Football League – and playing brilliantly – Hobson fell on his head and was carried off with concussion. Tom Galley, the Wolves wing-half, took on the goalkeeper's jersey and also played brilliantly. Billy Liddell of Liverpool joined the game as a substitute.

At half-time, the League led 3–2, but the second half brought 11 goals. Wags suggested that the cricket season had come a month early.

There is only space here to give the order of scoring: Stephenson (1–0 to the League), Nieuwenhuys (1–1), Dorsett (2–1 to the League), Cullis (2–2), Lawton (3–2 to the League), Busby (3–3), Lawton (4–3 to the League), Liddell (5–3), Fagan (5–4), Fagan (5–5), Hanson (6–5 to the League), Lawton (7–5), Stephenson own-goal (7–6), Dorsett (8–6), Stevenson (8–7) and Hanson (9–7 to the Football League).

It may be difficult to believe, but certain reporters at the game commented that it was only the goalkeepers who kept the scores down. And there is a rumour that a dour Lancastrian among the 15,000 crowd turned to his mate at the end of the game: 'Ee, lad, just think. It could easily have finished nowt-nowt.'

FARCE IN THE FOG

LONDON, NOVEMBER 1945

Moscow Dynamo's four-match tour of Britain attracted considerable publicity. The third match of the tour, against Arsenal, was unanimously described as a farce. It was played in a pea-soup fog at White Hart Lane, Tottenham – Arsenal's ground was still requisitioned for war use – and contained many disputes typical of matches between British teams and Continental opposition during that era. Post-match whining shifted between the Russian referee's system and decisions, the fouling, substitutions and, of course, the weather. In one afternoon the Russians were treated to a range of love-hate emotions.

The public became aware of a culture clash at the start of Dynamo's first match of the tour, against Chelsea, when each Russian player presented a bouquet of flowers to his opposite number. They drew that game 3–3, then beat Cardiff City 10–1 to set up an intriguing fixture with Arsenal. George Allison, Arsenal manager, included six guests in his team, the most famous being Stan Matthews and Stan Mortensen (both Blackpool) and Joe Bacuzzi (Fulham).

Fog muffles sound and destroys vision, and London in the 1940s provided regular experience. There is one story about a Charlton Athletic match being abandoned and the players lying in the bath before they realised goalkeeper Sam Bartram was not among them. They found him still in his goalmouth, hopping about, staying alert, thinking his team must be doing all the attacking.

The White Hart Lane farce shouldn't have started. According to the players, visibility was down to a yard or two. The Russian referee encouraged criticism by sticking to the Russian linear system of refereeing rather than the British diagonal system. The two British linesmen were on the same side of the pitch, helped a little by their luminous flags, a novelty in Britain.

Moscow Dynamo scored in the first minute but went 3–1 behind to goals by Ronnie Rooke and Stan Mortensen (2). At half-time Arsenal led 3–2.

Arsenal made a substitution at half-time – goalkeeper Brown for goalkeeper Williams – but later complained that Dynamo had substituted a player in the fog without anybody going off. There were also complaints that players from both sides were committing fouls and then sneaking back into the fog before the referee saw them. Considering visibility was so poor, people had amazing opinions of what was happening elsewhere on the pitch, such as the complaints about the last two Dynamo goals being offside or the shirt-pulling on Stan Matthews. Dynamo won 4–3, and, after the farce was completed, people agreed that the Russians were an excellent team, the best to visit Britain, a passing combination rather than individual dribblers. They went to Glasgow and drew 2–2 with Rangers before leaving.

Similar problems were faced by players during a wartime Edinburgh derby between Hibernian and Heart of Midlothian. Their fog-shrouded match should have been abandoned but it was continued so that German Luftwaffe pilots, listening to the improvised radio commentary, would think it was a clear day over Edinburgh.

THE 203-MINUTE GAME
STOCKPORT, MARCH 1946

No one had yet conceived penalty-kick deciders. When the Division Three North wartime Cup tie between Stockport County and Doncaster Rovers ended in a draw after extra-time, the two teams were asked to settle the outcome that day. The first team to score would win. But the scores were still level after 203 minutes when the game was abandoned through bad light.

The players were perhaps fortunate that the game didn't take place a month later. Had the clocks been on summer time, play might have lasted until eight o'clock.

The Cup tie had two legs. The first, at Doncaster, ended in a 2–2 draw. The second, at Stockport, finished with the same 2–2 scoreline. The competition rules dictated extra-time of ten minutes each way. This was played with no scoring. Then the teams played on until the first goal. Referee Baker of Crewe proved a hard taskmaster.

Three times Stockport's Ken Shaw had chances to add to the two goals he had scored in the first 90 minutes. Each time the chance went astray. The game went on and on. Stockport's Les Cocker (later trainer of Leeds United and England) put the ball into the Doncaster net but Mr Baker disallowed the point for an infringement.

There were 13,000 spectators at the game and most stayed until the end. Some went home for their tea and then came back again.

The teams toiled on. The sultry heat took its toll. After 200 minutes Stockport's Rickards tried a shot in the failing light. The ball cannoned off two Doncaster defenders and the goalkeeper. All three Rovers players were left laid out like ninepins. Eventually, after 203 minutes, the referee ended the endurance test. The two teams tossed a coin for choice of ground in the replay. Rovers won the toss and chose their own ground. The following Wednesday they beat Stockport 4–0.

WHEN TWO PLAYERS DIED
ALDERSHOT, APRIL 1948

Soccer can be a lethal game. The most common causes of football death have been serious head injuries (such as those received by the much-lamented Scottish international Jock Thomson), internal injuries (for instance, William Walker of Leith in 1907), pneumonia (e.g. Sam Wynne of Bury in 1927) and infections of wounds, particularly in the earlier years of the game, when internationals like Dunlop and Di Jones died in such circumstances.

More unusual fatal incidents have also occurred on the field. In 1897, Thomas Grice of Ashton, Cheshire, fell during a game and his belt buckle punctured his stomach. In Alicante, Spain, in 1924, the ball brought down a live electric wire and a player who went to remove it was electrocuted. James Beaumont was killed at Walkley, Sheffield, in 1877 when, chasing the ball, he jumped into a quarry.

Such accidents may happen, but clubs can plan emergency procedures, medical help and safety precautions to minimise their impact. Sometimes, though, death comes too suddenly, as was the case with the Army Cup Final replay of 1948.

The Cup Finalists were the Royal Armoured Corps (Bovington) and No. 121 Training Regiment of the Royal Artillery (Oswestry). Their first meeting, on Wednesday 14 April, was a 0–0 draw distinguished only by the presence of the King and Queen. The royal schedule was delayed by half an hour because extra-time was played.

The replay also took place at the Command Central Ground in Aldershot. Oswestry scored twice in the first 20 minutes and held their lead into the second half. A storm gathered some distance away. Rain was imminent. Forked lightning flashed its warning. The players took their positions for a throw-in on the opposite side to the grandstand. There was an electric flash of lightning and a simultaneous roar of thunder. The throw-in was never taken.

It was never known what attracted the lightning – some suggested the referee's whistle, others a water-pipe around the track – but the effect was devastating. Eight players and the referee swayed from side to side and then keeled over as though they had been hit on the back of the head. Two players died in the incident – 18-year-old Bertram Boardley, the left-half of the Oswestry team, and his direct opponent, Kenneth Hill of Bovington. The referee, Captain Green, who was on the Football League list, was detained in hospital that evening, and it was suggested that wearing rubber composition footwear might have helped him survive. Two other players and two spectators were also detained in hospital.

For about 30 seconds after the incident no one seemed to have understood what had happened. Then spectators and ambulance men began to move towards the injured. But virtually everyone was in a state of shock, and spectators commented on experiencing a tingling sensation. The game was abandoned and the two teams were given the Army Cup for six months each. The verdict on the dead men was 'death by misadventure, from heart failure, due to an electric shock from lightning'.

A similar event occurred in Birmingham in 1967. A Highgate United player was killed and seven players injured when they were struck by lightning during the FA Amateur Cup tie between Highgate and Enfield. The match was replayed at Villa Park and it was a very emotional occasion for the 32,000 spectators present.

DAYLIGHT ROBBERY
SCARBOROUGH, APRIL 1949

It is not unusual for thieves to raid a dressing-room while a game is in progress. My favourite story concerns a local game in the West Country. Two players, sent off by the referee, returned to the dressing-rooms when a robbery was taking place. They shouted the news, and all 22 players set off around the district to corner the robbers.

At Scarborough, on Easter Monday 1949, the thieves had an easier escape. The robbery took place during the first half, while Scarborough, third from bottom in the Midland League, were holding League leaders Gainsborough Trinity very creditably. The robbery was discovered at half-time. Money, wristwatches, cigarette lighters and fountain-pens were missing. The pockets of all the Scarborough players had been rifled, the referee and linesmen were victims too, and only the Gainsborough dressing-room was untouched. (Ah, Holmes, do you think this means it was a Gainsborough supporter? I think not, Watson.)

Scarborough goalkeeper Cyril Hannaby lost the key to his fish-and-chip shop in Doncaster and his return train ticket home. Bill Parke, the captain, lost his return ticket to York. Dennis Kirby lost his return ticket to Leeds. (Why, Holmes, the thieves must have split up after the robbery? Not necessarily, Watson.)

A tannoy announcement asked for Detective-Officer Bond, who was among the 3,500 crowd at the game.

There were few clues. No sign of a break-in. The thieves had probably sneaked in through the main doors and reached the dressing-room by the main passage. It was disconcerting for the Scarborough players, who had the second half to play. On the field they were robbed of victory too. After taking the lead late in the game, they conceded an own-goal with the last kick of the match. Scarborough's 1–1 draw was their best performance of the season, but it was an afternoon of mixed feelings.

'FOOTBALL'S MOST AMAZING EXPERIMENT'

HINCKLEY, APRIL 1949

There is a long-running football joke about a hypnotist who is called into a team's dressing-room to improve ailing performances. The hypnotist hasn't time to work on all the players so he singles out the jaded star striker (or, if you prefer, centre-forward). He puts his subject into a trance and tells him he has the sharpness of Gary Lineker, the strength of Maradona and the deadliness of Ian Rush (or, for those who remember, Denis Law, Geoff Hurst and Jimmy Greaves). The hypnotist snaps his fingers and tells the striker to change and go out to play the game of his life. 'Not bloody likely,' the player replies. 'I'm too good for this shower.'

Hypnotism has a powerful image. But does it work? Towards the end of the 1948–9 season, Hinckley Athletic, sliding towards the bottom of the Birmingham Combination, set up a publicity stunt which went a little wrong, mainly because the Hinckley directors blew hot and cold about the involvement of a hypnotist. It wasn't clear whether they were in favour or not.

The advertisement in the *Hinckley Times* was clear enough about the event scheduled for the Hinckley Working Men's Club Hall on Tuesday 12 April: 'Richard Payne will conduct an amazing experiment with members of the Hinckley Athletic team. Don't miss it.'

Richard Payne, billed as 'Britain's Greatest Hypnotist', was apparently taking an evening off from his billing at Leicester to do a special performance in aid of an improvement scheme for Hinckley Athletic's Middlefield Lane ground.

It was also expected that Payne would contribute to an improvement scheme for events on the pitch. Coming up in a week's time was a game against the leaders of the Birmingham Combination, local rivals Bedworth Town.

Three hundred fans turned up at the Working Men's Club Hall to see Richard Payne put six Hinckley Athletic players to sleep. 'You will win,' he told them. 'You will win.' It was mesmerising stuff. The left-half was so carried away that he kicked a hat a distance of 50 yards (45.7m) along the length of the hall. But the scheme had a second stage. Richard Payne planned to visit the Hinckley dressing-room on Easter Tuesday, the day of the big game against Bedworth. However, the directors weren't convinced a hypnotist was needed. They were thinking in terms of a new goalkeeper or a new player-manager. Payne failed to complete his project.

Although readers of the *Hinckley Times* were implored to visit Middlefield Lane on Easter Tuesday to assess the results of 'football's most amazing experiment', Richard Payne did not actually appear in the dressing-room, and Hinckley didn't play any better. Bedworth won 2–1 and clinched the Birmingham Combination Championship at a canter. Hinckley, in fact, lost all three Easter games and continued their downward trend. At the end of the season they parted company with player-coach Bobby Davidson. There is no record of whether any hypnotists applied for the vacant post.

THE INVISIBLE GAME
SOUTHAMPTON, OCTOBER 1950

When Southampton pioneered a floodlit exhibition match against neighbours Bournemouth, about 10,000 people took advantage of the offer of free admission, but they only just got their money's worth. It was a mysterious game that no one could see properly.

The idea emerged from Southampton's summer tour of Brazil, where they played several games under artificial light. The Southampton Supporters' club, on hearing the good reports, invested £600 for a firm called B.A. Corry to install 16 1,500-watt arc lamps. Everyone was pleasantly surprised that electricity running costs would be as low as six or seven shillings, so the big question was whether spectators would like it. Here was the big test.

Approaching kick-off time of 6.30p.m., the crowd began to gather and exchange wisecracks.

'Bring on the shadow teams.' 'Come on Wraith Rovers.' 'Pylon the pressure.'

The spectators had to rely on their own entertainment. Although the lights worked well, visibility was destroyed by a familiar British problem – fog. That evening the whole country was enveloped in a thick mist. At London Airport a BEA Viking airliner crashed, killing all 31 people aboard.

At Southampton's ground, the Dell, the fog wasn't too much of a handicap for the players, who could see the ball reasonably clearly, except when it was kicked high in the air, but the referee couldn't see a hand-ball in front of him, and the spectators were literally in the dark. At times visibility slumped to 3–4 yards (2.7–3.7m) and only nearside play could be seen.

The teams played for an hour, changing straight round without a half-time interval. For the spectators it was an eerie experience. In the damp night air, the Bournemouth players, wearing all-white, were a team of apparitions, flitting about like will-o'-the-wisps. From the stand, for all the crowd knew, the players could have been ghosts of the days when footballers wore moustaches and shin-pads outside socks – except for one two-minute period when the fog temporarily lifted and the outcome was theatrical.

There was a rumour that Southampton came close to scoring – Ken Bird pushed Eric Day's shot on to a goalpost – and the consensus was that the game finished without a goal. This was confirmed later by the players.

'Floodlit play needed infra-red glasses,' shrieked the *Daily Telegraph* headline the next day. Their reporter, Lainson Wood, was dubious about the future prospects of floodlights, saying that no one had made it pay in 20 years of dabbling, and there would always be fog.

Yet several onlookers were impressed.

'There were efforts to introduce floodlight football to this country before the war, but never anything so simple and economical as the installation at the Dell,' wrote Clifford Webb in the *Daily Herald*.

Another observer – if that is the right term for this fog-shrouded night – was Walter Winterbottom, the England team manager. 'This match,' Winterbottom was quoted as saying, 'has proved that even on a foggy night amateur players who cannot train in the daytime can get on to a pitch and have real match practice.'

Here, too, was the crux of Southampton's argument. Their chairman, Penn Barrow, pointed out that the cost of floodlights was far less than the cost of buying players. If they could produce one player from floodlight training it would have paid them.

This game, mysterious though it was to spectators, symbolised a new wave in the floodlighting movement. By the mid-1950s, lights were being used for games as well as for training.

TWO TEAMS, ONE MANAGER

YORK, OCTOBER 1952

Only a man like Dick Duckworth could manage two teams playing in the same game. His old club, York City, were playing his new club, Stockport County, and the game coincided with his changeover.

Dick Duckworth had an exceptionally long career as a player, manager and scout, serving more than a dozen Football League clubs. His playing career was mainly confined to Division Three North, although he helped Chesterfield to promotion and captained York City when they 'giant-killed' two First Division teams and Second Division Coventry City to reach the sixth round of the 1938 FA Cup competition. In between, Duckworth also played for Southport, Chester and Rotherham.

York City was Duckworth's first managerial job in the Football League. He had been there just over two years when he was offered a similar post at Stockport County, Andy Beattie having moved to Huddersfield Town. The York directors agreed to release Duckworth from his contract on 22 October 1952. His last game in charge was at home to Stockport County. The *Yorkshire Evening Press* described it as 'a piquant position for Mr Duckworth' and it certainly was. That week all the players on the field would come under his control.

Despite being third in Division Three North, York City were having difficulty scoring goals. Supporters writing to the local newspapers were suggesting the usual subtle tactical changes, like swapping the five forwards for those in the reserves. Dick Duckworth, a big, pipe-smoking, balding man with plenty of presence, wasn't the type to react to pressures from supporters, but, in his last week, he did bring in two reserves. Winger Bobby Warrender was introduced for his debut, and 18-year-old Dave Dunmore would play centre-forward against Stockport.

What must Dick Duckworth have thought when he saw York City overwhelm his new team? Billy Fenton scored twice and Dave Dunmore added a third, all in the first hour's play. York won 3–0, deservedly and decisively.

Duckworth learned that his new job would be a challenge. Stockport County, midway in the league table, had plenty of problems. Alf Lythgoe, who had followed Andy Beattie to Huddersfield, claimed that Stockport County were not a happy family and any new manager would have a tough job off the field. Twenty-seven Stockport players refuted this claim by signing an open letter: 'We, the undersigned players of Stockport County, resent the untrue statements under the name of Alf Lythgoe. To say that the County players are not a happy family off the field is a wicked insinuation. We are unanimous in giving the lie to this.'

In contrast to the youthful exuberance of York players like Dunmore, who was soon to attract a £10,000 cheque from Tottenham Hotspur, the Stockport County first team had an average age of 30.

Dick Duckworth never achieved promotion for Stockport County in his four years with the club, and his next club, Darlington, were similarly established in Division Three North. However, in his fourth Football League management job, Duckworth came close to achieving something no one had done and probably never will do. Any manager who can come within five Second Division points of taking Scunthorpe United into the First Division, as Duckworth did in 1961–2, deserves to manage both teams in more than one game.

THE 44-MINUTE GAME
COVENTRY, JANUARY 1956

If a player is sent off by the referee but refuses to leave the field then the referee should abandon the match. Arthur Ellis, an international referee from Halifax, did exactly that after 44 minutes of a floodlight friendly between Coventry City and San Lorenzo, an Argentinian club on tour in Britain.

Referring to tempestuous games as 'friendlies' is always a cheap joke, so perhaps the comparative American term 'exhibition game' is better suited. It was a real exhibition.

It started well enough and, as half-time approached, with the score 1–1, most people felt it had the potential to be a great game. Then Arthur Ellis, a Cup Final referee in 1952, awarded Coventry a penalty for a push on Dennis Uphill. Ellis was surrounded by Argentinians and kicked by teenage inside-left Jose Sanfilippo, who was sent off.

Sanfilippo refused to leave the field. Two team-mates tried to pull him off, three tried to keep him on. Interpreters, police and San Lorenzo officials were soon on the pitch. Arthur Ellis abandoned the match and stuck by his decision.

Coventry City chairman Erle Shanks had the task of announcing the news to the 17,000 crowd: 'Mr Ellis, the referee, states that he was kicked by the San Lorenzo player Sanfilippo. He immediately ordered the player to the dressing-room. The player refused to go and was supported in his attitude by certain of their players. Under the circumstances Mr Ellis has abandoned the game as he refuses to referee under these impossible conditions. Under FA rules we are not allowed to appoint a substitute.'

This was the fifth game of San Lorenzo's tour. They were finding it hard to adjust to the British mud and had yet to win. They had played Brentford, Rangers, Sheffield Wednesday, Wolves and now Coventry. Their sixth and last game was on a frozen pitch at Southampton, where San Lorenzo won 2–1. By that time San Lorenzo officials and Sanfilippo had apologised to Coventry City.

Jose Sanfilippo, whose stubbornness was described by Ellis as akin to that of a mule, had an interesting career. He was always scoring goals and always temperamental. He played for Argentina in the 1958 World Cup and was the country's top League goalscorer for four successive seasons (1958–61). Finally, San Lorenzo, finding him difficult to handle, transferred him to Boca Juniors for £85,000, the sort of money AC Milan were paying for Jimmy Greaves. Sanfilippo had success there, until he attacked the team coach. He moved on, continuing his chequered career until he returned to San Lorenzo in his late thirties. He had settled down by then.

SECOND-HALF TRANSFORMATION

LONDON, DECEMBER 1957

It was the Saturday before Christmas. Many of Charlton Athletic's regular supporters had opted for Christmas shopping rather than the home game against Huddersfield Town. Still more did the same after an hour's play. Charlton were losing 5–1 and were down to ten players. It didn't seem worth staying until the end. But let that be a warning. Those who left early missed a most amazing transformation.

Charlton Athletic's home, the Valley, was a huge stadium capable of holding 70,000, and on this pre-Christmas Saturday it looked fairly empty with only 12,500 spectators inside. At half-time Charlton were 2–0 down and not playing well. They had also lost centre-half Derek Ufton, who had dislocated a shoulder, and would have to play with ten men for the last 80 minutes of the game. No substitutes were allowed at that time.

The one man who will be forever associated with Charlton Athletic's stunning transformation that day was Johnny Summers, their tall, stocky outside-left. At half-time he changed his boots, thinking it would be a good time to break in a new pair. After all, Charlton had little chance, and his old pair of boots were falling to pieces.

In the third minute of the second half Summers scored his first goal, but Huddersfield Town popped in three more and led 5–1 after an hour. The visitors, who included future England full-back Ray Wilson and England international wing-half Bill McGarry, looked certainties for two Second Division points, even when John 'Buck' Ryan scored a consolation goal.

Then Johnny Summers scored four goals. In the rearrangements following Ufton's injury, Summers had moved to centre-forward. It was from this position that he scored his goals, all with his unnatural right foot, all wearing his new boots. The remaining spectators were rewarded for their loyalty. They were going berserk and there were still ten minutes to play, Charlton leading 6–5. Then Huddersfield equalised.

The winning goal came with the last shot of the match. Charlton's Fred Lucas fed John Ryan and the big attacker slammed the eleventh goal of the second half. Charlton had won 7–6. Moments later, when the final whistle went, the crowd began calling for the players and Johnny Summers in particular. 'We want Summers,' they chanted. At length the players appeared in the directors' box, and were greeted rapturously.

Meanwhile, in the Miller Hospital at Greenwich, the injured Derek Ufton could hardly believe what he was hearing, 7–6? It couldn't have been the game he started off in. It wasn't until team-mate Stuart Leary visited him at the hospital that Ufton could take in the news.

There was a strange sequel less than three weeks later. Charlton Athletic and Huddersfield Town met in an FA Cup third-round replay at the same place, the Valley. A much bigger crowd turned out, expecting a repeat of the goal glut. Charlton won 1–0.

THE TRIPLICATED CUP TIE

LEEDS, JANUARY 1958

In 1955–6, in the third round of the FA Cup, Leeds United were drawn at home to Cardiff City.

In 1956–7, in the third round of the FA Cup, Leeds United were drawn at home to Cardiff City.

In 1957–8, in the third round of the FA Cup, Leeds United were drawn at home to Cardiff City.

Had the possibility been suggested before the 1955–6 third-round draw that Leeds would be at home to Cardiff in three successive seasons, a statistician would have calculated the odds at one in two million. Yet something even more unlikely occurred. Let's look at the results.

In 1955–6, Cardiff City won 2–1 at Leeds after a goalless first half.

In 1956–7, Cardiff City won 2–1 at Leeds after a goalless first half.

In January 1958, therefore, there was a sense of *déjà vu* when 30,374 people visited Elland Road, Leeds, to see the third third-round meeting in successive seasons. Surely Leeds must now gain revenge. The status of the clubs had been reversed. Whereas Cardiff were in the First Division and Leeds in the Second in January 1956, the roles were now the opposite, Leeds promoted, Cardiff relegated. When the teams had met in the First Division, in 1956–7, Leeds had cruised to a 3–0 home victory. It was virtually impossible for three successive 2–1 away wins to occur.

Or was it?

The conditions were icy and precarious. Second Division Cardiff scored first, Alan Harrington scoring from long range in the twentieth minute. Bobby Forrest equalised with a header from Wilbur Cush's centre and Leeds took control. Right on half-time, however, came a second Cardiff goal, Cliff Nugent being the scorer. At half-time Cardiff led by the magic, magnetic 2–1 scoreline.

Surely it couldn't happen again – but it did. The referee had the best chance to prevent a 2–1 Cardiff win, when, in the last minute, Wilbur Cush was brought down and Leeds appealed for a penalty. It was not given. Cardiff won 2–1 – three times in a row.

GIANT-KILLING GLORY
WORCESTER, JANUARY 1959

A director of a Fourth Division club once arrived at the stadium on the afternoon of a home tie against attractive First Division opposition. He surveyed the 'icebergs' and ruts at one end of the pitch and the mud and straw at the other and gave his opinion about the obvious postponement. 'Get the referee to play it,' he told the secretary. 'We can beat them on this.'

Ah, the beauty of the British weather in January, the glory of the FA Cup. No book on strange matches would be complete without at least one giant-killing act, where a small club produces an odd result against a big club.

Not all giant-killing, however, is strange. Some teams, like Peterborough United and Swindon Town in the 1960s, were so good at it that people turned up expecting an upset. Some had such good giant-killing years that they almost went the distance. One thinks of Millwall (1937), Port Vale (1954), York City (1955), Norwich City (1959) and Crystal Palace (1976), all of whom reached the semi-final. Certain top clubs create a reputation for being vulnerable. Newcastle United may have won three post-war FA Cup Finals but they have also lost home draws to a galaxy of lower-division teams – Bradford Park Avenue, Rotherham, Scunthorpe, Peterborough, Bedford Town, Carlisle United, Hereford United (in a replay), Wrexham (in a replay), Chester and Exeter City (in a replay). In a year when they did get to

Wembley (1974), Newcastle started their Cup run by drawing 1–1 at home to Hendon. The result was almost predictable.

One of the glamorous features about the FA Cup is that it can create fixtures which are strange (whatever the result): Tooting & Mitcham against Nottingham Forest (1959), Ashington against Aston Villa (1924), Manchester United against Walthamstow Avenue (1953), Lovell's Athletic against Wolverhampton Wanderers (1946), and so on. When a non-League team beats First Division opposition it is front-page news – for instance, Colchester United against Huddersfield (1948), Yeovil against Sunderland (1949), Hereford against Newcastle (1972) and Sutton United against Coventry City (1989).

I have chosen a third-round FA Cup tie on the edge of that pack, one perhaps less remembered, but which, in my opinion, captures the essence of the FA Cup and the vagaries of the British weather. Southern League Worcester City were hosts to Second Division promotion favourites Liverpool, who had lost only two of their last 16 games. Ground conditions for the Saturday of the game were typical Cup-tie conditions. Worcester cleared the snow from the pitch, which then froze. The referee postponed the game.

They tried again the following Thursday. Liverpool had to return tickets they couldn't sell and Worcester City sold them. The crowd was more partisan, the pitch still frozen, the ball erratic in its bounce and not easy to control. In the tenth minute Liverpool full-back John Molyneux tried a back-pass, goalkeeper Tommy Younger did his best to reach it, Worcester's 18-year-old Tommy Skuse skated after it, put the ball in the net and promptly fell over.

Worcester's second goal, in the eighty-second minute, was just as unfortunate for the Liverpool defence. Harry Knowles crossed hard from the right, Liverpool centre-half Dick White kicked at the centre and the ball flew over goalkeeper Younger for an own-goal. A minute later

Liverpool pulled back a goal, Geoff Twentyman scoring from a penalty.

The last few minutes seemed like hours to Worcester fans. When the final whistle went, the score still 2–1, they swarmed on to the field to congratulate their heroes, throwing hats in the air, engulfing the blue-and-white-shirted players, lifting up goalkeeper Johnny Kirkwood and captain Roy Paul and carrying them from the field. Paul had captained Manchester City when they won the 1956 FA Cup Final.

Worcester City manager Bill Thompson, who had made a few appearances for Portsmouth in the Championship-winning seasons of 1948–9 and 1949–50, could feel proud of his team's gritty performance. The pitch aside, Worcester had played determinedly and won deservedly. That season Worcester set three record attendances for the St George's Lane ground, the first against Millwall in the second round, the last when Sheffield United won 2–0 in the fourth round. Their Cup run should be remembered for the day Worcester City inflicted one of the strangest defeats in Liverpool's history.

THE MISSING FUSES

WATFORD, APRIL 1959

There are several games in which floodlight failure has led to long delays or even abandonments, but perhaps one of the most mysterious was the Watford-Shrewsbury clash close to the end of the 1958–9 season.

Shrewsbury Town were challenging for promotion, occupying fourth place in the new Fourth Division, but they had little to spare and were closely scrutinising the goal average of fifth-placed Exeter City. Two days after this Watford game, Shrewsbury would face Exeter at home.

Watford, a mid-table team, had little to play for except the end of the season. At half-time they were losing 4–1 to Shrewsbury, having conceded two own-goals on a pitch which was hard, bumpy and of unpredictable bounce.

Halfway through the second half the floodlights suddenly went off. It transpired later that three fuses had been removed. Not a case of sabotage, the police believed, more a case of larceny.

It was an evening game. There was still some natural light, but not enough. Nevertheless, referee Denis Howell started the game again. Meanwhile, club officials tried to do what they could with the floodlights, a bit daunting given the notice on the doors: 'Danger, high voltage electricity'.

Fuse thieves must know what they are doing.

The pitch was virtually in darkness, but the teams did their best to play on. Spectators tried to help by lighting newspapers. Watford's Peter Walker shot from 35 yards (32m) and nobody thought to warn Shrewsbury goalkeeper Russell Crossley that a ball was on its way. It flew past him into the net. Then Colin Whitaker scored one at the other end. Shrewsbury led 5–2, but conditions were impossible. Recognising the risk of injury, referee Howell abandoned the game after 76 minutes.

Shrewsbury claimed it was floodlight robbery as they needed those two points and five goals for their promotion prospects. The Watford club was fined £100 by the Football League for failing to ensure their floodlights were in order. The game had to be played again. The Football League said it should be played in daylight hours.

When Shrewsbury returned to Watford in the first week in May, having meantime beaten Exeter City by three goals from player-manager Arthur Rowley, they needed a point to guarantee promotion. There was a sense of justice about the result. Shrewsbury beat Watford 4–1, exactly the score when the floodlights failed in the previous abandoned game. They were promoted to Division Three, where they stayed for the next 15 seasons.

'FANTASTIC, INCREDIBLE, AMAZING'

LONDON, OCTOBER 1960

Cliff Mitchell, sports reporter on the Middlesbrough *Evening Gazette*, ran out of superlatives when describing the Division Two game between Charlton Athletic and Middlesbrough: 'Fantastic, incredible, amazing ... it was rumbustious, dynamic fare and it stirred the blood ... I can't imagine a more thrilling tussle than this one. It will live for years.'

All the ingredients were right. It was early enough in the season for teams to be carefree, energetic and optimistic. The relentless rain produced a slippery grassy surface which encouraged a fast pace. Both teams were in goalscoring form – Charlton had won 5–3 at Brighton the previous week, Middlesbrough had recently chalked up high-scoring draws at Leeds (4–4) and Plymouth (3–3) – and both clubs had a goal-scoring tradition. Charlton had averaged almost 100 goals a season since they slipped into Division Two in 1957, Middlesbrough had scored over 80 goals in each of their last four seasons.

There were also some special goalscorers in action. Brian Clough, Middlesbrough's England-international centre-forward, maintained a phenomenal strike rate. The player alongside him, Alan Peacock, would also play for England and command a high transfer fee from Leeds United. Charlton had two men, Stuart Leary and Johnny Summers, who would end their careers with over 150 Football League goals.

There were enough incidents in the first 13 minutes to satisfy many crowds for a whole game. Yet there were no goals from this hectic start. Once the teams started scoring the game went out of control. Eleven goals in 54 minutes: Eddie Werge (1–0 to Charlton after 13), Brian Clough (1–1 after 15), Ron Burbeck (2–1 to Middlesbrough after 17), Dennis Edwards (2–2 after 21), Stuart Leary (3–2 to Charlton after 28), Derek McLean (3–3 after 29), Clough again (4–3 to Middlesbrough after 30), Edwards again (4–4 at half-time), Burbeck (5–4 to Middlesbrough after 49), Clough for his hat-trick (6–4 after 63), Edwards for his hat-trick (6–5 to Middlesbrough after 69 minutes).

The finale was saved for the last minute. Johnny Summers dropped a centre in the Middlesbrough goalmouth. A swarm of muddy players challenged hungrily. Somehow the ball ended in the net without touching anyone. A real old-fashioned goal to end a real old-fashioned game. Six goals each. Fantastic, incredible, amazing.

THE DISALLOWED
DOUBLE HAT-TRICK
LUTON, JANUARY 1961

On a day of relentless rain, on a pitch of mainly mud, Denis Law scored six successive goals in 50 minutes to help Manchester City into a 6–2 lead against Luton Town. Unfortunately for Law and Manchester City, the referee abandoned the game after 69 minutes. Luton and Manchester City had to start their fourth-round FA Cup tie again the following Wednesday.

The first meeting had plenty of twists. After 17 minutes Luton were 2–0 ahead, Alec Ashworth scoring both. Then came Law's spectacular show. The Scottish international showed incredible close-range reactions as he headed and flicked in anything that was in the goal-area, taking advantage of defenders floundering in the mud. One hat-trick was followed by another, but, all the time, there were doubts about the pitch. Finally, after 69 minutes, referee Ken Tuck of Chesterfield abandoned the game.

The second attempt started similarly to the first, Luton scoring twice in the first 22 minutes. Denis Law scored for Manchester City just before half-time, but this time there were no hat-tricks to follow. Ashworth's second-half goal sealed a 3–1 victory for Luton, although, overall, Manchester City had scored seven (Law seven) and Luton only five (Ashworth four and Fleming one).

Luton lost 1–0 at Third Division Barnsley in the fifth round.

THE NIGHTMARE DAY-TRIP

BARROW, OCTOBER 1961

Gillingham thought they could travel to Barrow on the day of the game. The journey from the mouth of Kent's River Medway to the tip of the Furness peninsula in Lancashire (as it was then) was over 300 miles (483km). A train leaving London Euston at 9.05a.m. seemed a safe bet. The team should arrive over an hour before kick-off, which was at 5.15p.m. as Barrow had no floodlights.

First came the 35-mile (56.3-km) coach trip to Euston. The coach made an early-morning start but ran into heavy traffic and officials grew agitated. The coach arrived at Euston half an hour after the train had left.

The options remaining were not promising. The next train, the 10.25, would arrive one minute after the kick-off. Coach would be too slow, and cars would be very risky. There was only possibility – aeroplane. Club officials discovered two suitable scheduled flights – the 10.40 to Manchester and the 11.00 to Newcastle. Both were fully booked.

The next idea was to charter a plane. One was arranged but the company had to fly it from Gatwick to London Airport, where the Gillingham party would be waiting. The cost of the plane was £500 – money in advance.

Gillingham officials also telephoned the Football League. They negotiated a 15-minute delay in kick-off time. The players would be asked to forgo their half-time interval. It was now a 5.30p.m. kick-off.

The next problem was the plane's destination. They decided to head for Squire's Gate Airport at Blackpool, about 70 miles (113km) from Barrow. This meant arranging another journey. A coach was hired to meet them at Squire's Gate, but, as time slipped by, officials realised a coach would be too slow. Four cars were hired and a police escort arranged for what would be a hectic last leg of the trip.

The charter flight left London Airport at 2.31p.m., having been delayed in a queue of planes. There were less than three hours before the match.

The plane arrived at Squire's Gate at 3.25. Within 20 minutes everybody was in cars. They had a 70-mile (113-km) journey and 105 minutes.

There were no motorways in the north-west in October 1961. The roads around Morecambe Bay were among the country's worst for a late dash by car through driving rain. They reached Holker Street at 5.30p.m. The players needed to change.

Gillingham, as you can appreciate, were not ideally prepared to play a Fourth Division game. They'd been up early, stuck in traffic on a coach, forced to hang around, shepherded on to a plane (the first time for some), driven rapidly through the countryside and told to change as quickly as they could. By half-time they were five goals down to Barrow.

The problem now was the light. By the seventy-fourth minute, when Barrow were leading 6–0, referee Mr Jobling from Morecambe felt it was too dark for football. He allowed an extra couple of minutes under Barrow's training lights – just time for Barrow's seventh goal – but finally abandoned the game shortly after seven o'clock.

The Football League ruled that the 7–0 scoreline should stand as a result. Gillingham's next away game was an even longer trip – Carlisle United. They set off in good time and won 2–1.

FAREWELL IN A BLIZZARD

CREWE, MARCH 1962

Crewe in the snow. It seemed like the last place on earth, and it was, literally, for the visitors. A few days later Accrington Stanley died. This was the club's final fixture.

As a game, it was ordinarily one-sided. Crewe's Terry Tighe, a former Accrington player, sportingly did his best to give his former club a first-minute boost – his back-pass was cleared off the goal-line – but thereafter it was one-way traffic towards the Accrington goal. Probably the coldest man in Crewe that day was Jack Ferguson, the home-team goalkeeper, who was stranded alone in a snowstorm as Crewe scored four times at the other end.

Accrington Stanley were saved from an even bigger defeat than 4–0 by goalkeeper Alex Smith, who, according to one report, was in 'the £15,000 class' (not far below the £23,500 Harry Gregg goalkeeping record) and whose penalty save at Doncaster in the previous game had earned Accrington Stanley their last-ever Fourth Division point. Smith nearly didn't play at Crewe, relying on a late dash by car to join the team at Knutsford after missing the team coach. He had just moved into a new house and must have been looking forward to a career with his new club. A few days later he was out of a job.

On the Monday after the Friday game at Crewe, Accrington Stanley held a meeting of creditors. The news was worse than anyone had anticipated. Unsecured creditors were owed over £43,000 (more than the cost of Brian Clough's big news transfer from Middlesbrough to Sunderland around the same time) and the club had total debts of around £60,000. Accrington Stanley could no longer compete with the seven Lancashire clubs in the First Division. Stanley resigned from the Football League. The league had lost one of its founder members.

The directors had been paying players' wages for many months. Now they needed an immediate £400 to prevent the cutting-off of telephone, gas, electricity and water. When the players reported on Tuesday they were told the sad news, but no training was possible anyway – the water pipes were frozen. The players stood around and kicked their heels while a tradesman's van came to collect the club's washing-machine.

After three days of mourning there was another attempt to resurrect the club with yet another 'Save Stanley' campaign. There was no success. The Football League refused to rescind Accrington Stanley's resignation. The club had played its last game on a snowy, eerie night in Crewe.

ALL IN THE IMAGINATION
FORFAR, FEBRUARY 1963

'It was a great game at Station Park on Saturday although few spectators braved the elements. Three seagulls and a dead sparrow occupied the enclosure, while the only spectator in the stand besides the "Dispatch" reporter was a dispossessed field-mouse.'

That was how the *Forfar Dispatch* introduced its report of the imaginary game between Forfar Athletic and Stirling Albion during the big-freeze winter of 1962–3. Snow and ice layered the pitches and terraces, matches were postponed *en masse* and a major casualty was the football pools, until the introduction of a pools panel to fix the results of imaginary games.

The pools companies first disclosed the plan in the third week of January. If there were more than 30 postponements a panel of experts would forecast results of games postponed – home win, away win or draw. (In the 1960s, 0–0 draws counted the same as other draws in pools points.) Doubts about the legality of the scheme were overcome and a panel brought into action. It consisted of Lord Brabazon of Tara (chair) and four ex-international players, Ted Drake, Tom Finney, Tommy Lawton and George Young.

The objectives of the scheme were very clear – to help the pools companies and provide a continuing outlet for the nation's gambling impulses. This was little consolation for non-gambling soccer fans, who had no chance of following a game ... unless they read the *Forfar Dispatch*. The reporter took the panel's imaginary result and unearthed an imaginary game which was exciting from the very start.

'Straight from the first blast of the imaginary referee's kid-on whistle, Albion swept into the attack. Lawlor, scrambling over a large heap of salt in the Forfar goal-area, got his boot to a loose ball but kicked it high over the bar. Play was held up for five minutes while the luckless inside-right, assisted by his team-mates, searched for his boot in the adjacent field.'

You get the idea?

You are given the result – in this case an away win to Stirling Albion – and you write the match report to fit the result. I'm surprised more reporters don't try it.

The *Forfar Dispatch* spared us no details. We learn about the first goal – scored by Park while the Forfar goalkeeper had his foot caught in the side-netting – and the three incidents needing the non-existent trainer's magic sponge: Dick shot over the bar and landed heavily when he came down on the other side; Cumming, in agony, pink in the face, clutching his stomach, needed a new piece of elastic for his shorts; and a Forfar forward, through on his own, hit the post, and was carried off with a nasty bump on his forehead.

Reid scored Forfar's equaliser – his colleagues pelted the Stirling goalkeeper with snowballs – and it was 1–1 at the end of the first half, which lasted for 63 minutes as the referee had difficulty defrosting the pea in his whistle.

Both teams scored early in the second half. Soon Forfar led by the odd goal in five, and a very odd goal it was, scored by Dick, who tied his boot-lace to the football-lace and ran 50 yards (45.7m) into the net. An excellent imaginary pass by Stirling's Fish started Stirling's recovery. They went 4–3 ahead but Forfar equalised. 4–4. Time running out. The *Forfar Dispatch* captured those last tense moments with typical brilliance: 'Forfar officials were already on the phone to London to tell the panel of pools experts that the game was an imaginary draw when, in the dying minutes, Johnstone notched up number five for the visitors, a kid-on away win.'

The reporter added a footnote about the Stirling Albion defender who, on hearing his team had been awarded an away win, went to his manager and asked for his win bonus. 'Surely, I must have told you,' said the quick-thinking manager. 'You were dropped for that game.'

All fiction, perhaps, but this imaginary game had its roots in the reality of a pools-panel away win. From the town that had once provided one of football's most alliterative 5–4 results – Forfar five East Fife four (try saying that in a hurry) – now came the most vivid account of an imaginary 5–4 result. And, just for the record, the pools panel had it correct. When the teams met later in the season Stirling Albion recorded an away win. The score, though, was 2–0.

THE ABANDONED INTERNATIONAL

GLASGOW, MAY 1963

The Scotland–Austria international match at Hampden Park, watched by over 94,000 people, began to simmer in the sixteenth minute when Davie Wilson scored for Scotland. Austrian players had noticed the linesman's raised flag. Referee Jim Finney waved aside their protests.

After Wilson's second goal, ten minutes later, Austrian centre-forward Nemec was sent off for protesting too much. That left ten Austrians against eleven Scots, and the Scots led 2–0 in goals. By half-time Denis Law added a third goal.

Early in the second half, Austria lost the injured Rafreider, who was taken from the field on a stretcher. The teams had agreed to substitute outfield players until half-time and goalkeepers at any time. Rafreider was an outfield player. That left nine Austrians against eleven Scots, and the Scots led 3–0 in goals.

Denis Law scored a fourth Scotland goal, his second of the game. Linhart scored one for Austria. Then came another unsavoury incident. Hof was sent off for a violent tackle. That left eight Austrians against eleven Scots, and the Scots led 4–1 in goals.

After more eruptions referee Finney decided he had had enough. He abandoned the game after 79 minutes, not wanting anyone else to be hurt. After all, it was a 'friendly'.

THE GAME IN TWO GROUNDS

CARDIFF AND COVENTRY, OCTOBER 1965

The Football League Division Two game between Cardiff City and Coventry City, watched by 12,639 people in Cardiff and 10,295 people in Coventry, was the first of its kind in Britain. It was relayed by closed-circuit television.

Immediately after Coventry's reserve game on Tuesday evening, the day before the game at Cardiff, workmen went into action at Highfield Road to erect scaffolding and four large screens, each 40ft (12.2m) by 30ft (9.1m). Three screens faced the Sky Blue Stand, Coventry's main stand. Work went on through the night and was completed minutes before the 7.30p.m. kick-off at Cardiff.

The technical details, arranged by Intertel and Viewsport, were a success. The commentary was conducted by John Camkin, a journalist and Coventry City director, and Danny Blanchflower, former Spurs captain and a *Sunday Express* columnist. Coventry City obligingly switched to a set of red-and-white striped shirts, borrowed from Stoke City, to provide a more distinct contrast with Cardiff shirts.

The crowd at Highfield Road cheered as loudly as that at Ninian Park, especially when George Curtis gave Coventry the lead shortly before half-time.

During the second half, fog hung around Highfield Road, but the spectators were rarely distracted. Cardiff equalised through Gareth Williams in the fifty-fifth minute and Coventry's hopes of a first away win of the season lessened.

Then, three minutes from the end, Coventry scored the winner, a low shot from Welshman Ronnie Rees.

It was an exciting time in Coventry. Students were arriving at the new University of Warwick, and Coventry City were pushing towards Division One under the idea-laden leadership of manager Jimmy Hill and chairman Derrick Robins. Everything was Sky Blue – the Sky Blue Stand, the Sky Blue Train, the Sky Blue Shop, Radio Sky Blue, Sky Blue Caterers, the Sky Blue Song and, of course, Sky Blue Shirts.

Sky Blue closed-circuit television was the latest success, but the games would require very careful selection, needing to be between clubs some distance apart, so that away fans would not be prevented from travelling, and in order not to clash with other matches nearby. That would leave two or three midweek games a season at the most.

A PAIR OF BROKEN LEGS

CHESTER, JANUARY 1966

One of soccer's strangest coincidences occurred on New Year's Day 1966 when Chester full-backs Ray Jones and Bryn Jones both broke their left legs in the home game with Aldershot.

There were four players called Jones on the pitch that fateful day – Les was a Chester forward and David was the Aldershot goalkeeper – and, by the fifty-fifth minute, when the second injury happened, the others must have been wondering about their destinies.

The first accident occurred in the twenty-first minute. Bryn Jones tackled Derek Norman as the Aldershot forward carried the ball away. Jones was lying injured when Aldershot's Tony Priscott headed the game's opening goal. But the goal was followed by a bizarre incident – two Aldershot players seemingly fighting each other. Aldershot manager Dave Smith later explained that Norman thought he was being attacked by a Chester player rather than congratulated by a team-mate. Bryn Jones was treated for his leg fracture and taken to hospital.

Chester, with David Read on as substitute, took the initiative and showed why they were chasing promotion from the Fourth Division. Hugh Ryden scored two goals, including a 30-yard (27.4-m) shot, and Chester had a 2–1 half-time lead.

Aldershot's Ken Maloy equalised five minutes after half-time. Then came the second tragedy of the day. Ray Jones broke his leg making a tackle, and the next time the two Chester full-backs lined up together was in a hospital ward. On the pitch, Chester, now with ten men, contrived a memorable winning goal for Mick Metcalf.

Despite this 3–2 success, Chester's promotion challenge began to fall away. They were handicapped by the loss of their two regular full-backs for the rest of the season, and were left to digest the peculiarities of the Aldershot game when both full-backs, both called Jones, both broke their left legs.

THE POPULAR
NORTH KOREANS
LIVERPOOL, JUNE 1966

Some people thought it ridiculous that a team of no-hopers like North Korea could be allowed to qualify for the 1966 World Cup Finals, whereas other, more proven nations, like Czechoslovakia, Yugoslavia and Scotland, would not be there. Nobody who followed the World Cup Finals in England stuck to that opinion.

North Korea predictably lost to Russia in their first game, but gained a 1–1 draw with Chile from a late equaliser. But in the final match in their group a goal from Pak Du-ik beat Italy, the group favourites. The Italians, surprisingly eliminated, did their best to sneak back home at one o'clock in the morning, at an unscheduled airfield, but their players were still hit by a torrent of tomatoes.

North Korea's progress to the quarter-final set up an astonishing match with Portugal, one of the most sporting and delightfully entertaining teams of the tournament. Portugal were also one of the favourites for the trophy, bristling with talented players like Simoes, Eusebio and Torres, the latter's height expected to provide problems for the North Koreans, none of whom were over 5ft 8in (1.7m) tall.

After 24 minutes the North Koreans led 3–0, a dazzling display of bustling, intricate short-passing football with powerful finishing. The Goodison Park crowd took them to their hearts just as those at Middlesbrough had during the group matches.

The game was transformed by Eusebio. Born and raised in Mozambique, a Portuguese colony until 1975, Eusebio had developed into one of the world's stars and was at his peak in this World Cup, if not this game. Dubbed the European Pelé, or the Black Panther, by British newspapers, he had a superb physique, electrifying pace, a deft dribbling touch and a vicious shot. He showed it all this day.

Before half-time Eusebio scored twice, one virtually on his own, the other a penalty. Urgently, he picked the ball out of the net, ran with it back to the centre spot and handed it over, aware that Portugal had time and goals to make up. Eusebio equalised on the hour and scored his fourth from a penalty, taken with typical power. He made the fifth for Augusta. Portugal won 5–3.

The idea of two foreign international teams playing at Goodison Park was strange, that one of them should be North Korea was downright peculiar, but the outcome was memorable.

THE FANTASTIC
CHAMPIONSHIP DECIDER
LOS ANGELES, JULY 1967

When Wolverhampton Wanderers (alias Los Angeles Wolves) met Aberdeen (alias Washington Whips) in a decider for the United Soccer Association Championship, the game lasted 126 minutes. There were 11 goals, including four in one three-minute spell, a sending-off and three penalties. Wolves manager Ron Allen was quoted in one newspaper as saying it was the most fantastic match he had ever seen.

This was the climax of an eventful and controversial season when promoters thought they could establish soccer in the United States. Their hopes were based on American interest when the 1966 World Cup Finals were televised. Indeed, a game between Santos (Brazil) and Inter-Milan (Italy) brought 41,598 spectators to New York's Yankee Stadium in September 1966.

In 1967 there were two rival leagues operating in the United States. The outlawed National Professional Soccer League (NPSL) had ten clubs, each importing players from a variety of countries. Philadelphia needed to employ a full-time interpreter, while spectators were asked to support strangers, some with names which looked better suited to a optician's eye-chart.

One month into the season the NPSL was averaging only 5,000 spectators per game and was having problems with television coverage. In order to guarantee bursts of advertising every few minutes, the games needed unnatural breaks. Referees were accused of faking fouls to generate a necessary stoppage.

The United Soccer Association, which cunningly abbreviated to USA, was the more successful league. A dozen established clubs, invited from South America and Europe, were asked to pose under American names. They played in two sections (East and West) and the Championship decider would see the two section leaders meet. This is how Aberdeen (sorry, Washington Whips) came to play Wolves (Los Angeles Wolves) in the Memorial Coliseum Stadium on 14 July.

The USA season had not been without its problems. The game between Detroit Cougars (Glentoran of Northern Ireland) and Houston Stars (Bangu of Brazil) was abandoned after 73 minutes as players and spectators fought on the field. And when the New York Skyliners (Cerro of Uruguay) played the Cleveland Stokers (Stoke City of England) police were called in to separate brawling players. Fortunately, the Championship decider would be remembered for its entertainment value.

Wolves and Aberdeen had already met in a mini-league fixture. After a 1–1 draw, an Aberdeen protest was upheld – Wolves manager Ronnie Allen had used three outfield substitutes whereas the rules stated two plus a goalkeeper – and the Scottish club won the replay 3–0. This game could not be taken as a form guide as Wolves players were probably hung-over from their success in winning the Western Division. No one could have predicted the events of the East-West Championship decider.

Peter Knowles (Wolves) and Jim Smith (Aberdeen) scored early goals, but it was not until an hour's play that the game erupted. During a dramatic four-minute period, David Burnside of Wolves twice scored equalisers, cancelling out goals by Frank Munro and Jim Storrie.

When Aberdeen's Jim Smith was sent off in the eightieth minute, and then David Burnside put Wolves ahead, the game looked lost for Aberdeen. But Frank Munro made it 4–4 with a last-minute penalty. Extra-time was necessary.

Derek Dougan gave Wolves a 5–4 lead and again Aberdeen looked a beaten team, especially when Terry Wharton stepped up to take a Wolves penalty with only a few minutes to play. Goalkeeper Bobby Clark saved the penalty, Aberdeen won their own penalty, and, for the second time in the match, Frank Munro scored a last-minute equaliser. At 5–5, the rules called for sudden-death overtime. The first team to score would win. The winning goal came in the one hundred and twenty-sixth minute. British reporters referred to it as an own-goal, but the *New York Times* was more gracious, assigning the term 'accidental goal'. Wolves full-back Bobby Thomson escaped down the left wing, his cross deceived Clark and the ball bounced off Ally Shewin's thigh into the open goal. The crowd was stunned for a moment, then they realised that Wolves had won. The Championship was theirs, although Ronnie Allen sportingly suggested that the fairest thing after such a game would be to chop the trophy in half. They should award trophies for strangeness.

A TOUCH OF MAYHEM
MONTEVIDEO, NOVEMBER 1967

Celtic, European Cup holders, played Racing Club of Argentina, South America Cup winners, for the championship of the world. Celtic won 1–0 in Glasgow, Racing won 2–1 in Buenos Aires. The play-off was in Uruguay.

Some people suspected there would be trouble. Before the game in Buenos Aires, Celtic goalkeeper Ronnie Simpson was hit on the head by a missile, and John Fallon was hastily substituted. Tension had been building up, and, when the play-off started, referee Rodolfo Perez Oserio from Paraguay soon knew it would be one of his most difficult games. In the twenty-fifth minute he called together the two captains and issued a warning.

One man receiving plenty of rough treatment was Celtic winger Jimmy Johnstone, a tiny, jinking player, whose natural game was to take on defenders in tight spaces. In the thirty-seventh minute Johnstone was fouled by Rulli, and Celtic players rushed in to protect their winger. Fights broke out and next it was the police's turn to rush in and do some protecting.

After a five-minute delay, Basile (Racing) and Lennox (Celtic) were sent off. The brawl continued with ten a side. By half-time Celtic had conceded 24 fouls and Racing ten.

In the forty-eighth minute, Jimmy Johnstone, fouled yet again, retaliated by hitting Martin. Johnstone was sent off,

Celtic were a man short and, eight minutes later, Cardenas scored for Racing, the first goal of the game.

John Hughes was the next to go, sent off for a blatant foul on the Racing goalkeeper. Celtic's chances of saving the game seemed to have completely disappeared, although Racing's Rulli was sent off with four minutes to play. That left eight Celtic players against nine of Racing.

With two minutes to play another free-for-all broke out, and it was a wonder the game was ever finished. The referee implied he had sent off Celtic's Bertie Auld, but the Celtic man was still on the field at the end. By then there was nothing but confusion. And television coverage, claimed by some to be ghoulish, added to the débâcle. Never before had so many players been sent off in a game involving a professional British team.

THE REFEREE'S WINNING GOAL

BARROW, NOVEMBER 1968

Barrow 0, Plymouth Argyle 0, 13 minutes to play. Then came a goal to settle this Division Three game, scored by the most unlikely person on the pitch – referee Ivan Robinson.

Barrow won a corner-kick. The ball was cleared out. George McLean shot hard from outside the penalty area and the ball was going well wide. Referee Robinson, perhaps 15 yards (13.7m) from goal, was in the ball's path. He jumped up to avoid the ball but it hit him on the inside of his left foot and flew off at an angle. Plymouth goalkeeper Pat Dunne was completely deceived by the deflection. Having moved to cover McLean's shot, Dunne was stranded as the ball shot past him into the net. Barrow 1 (the Referee), Plymouth 0.

The rules are quite clear. The ball is in play if it rebounds off either the referee or linesmen when they are in the field of play. Ivan Robinson knew that. He pointed meekly to the centre-circle to confirm his goal. Plymouth players looked stunned and shocked. The incident spurred Plymouth into a frenzied late rally. Barrow hung on to win 1–0 and the referee had to try to avoid congratulatory pats on the back from Barrow supporters as he ran off the field.

Barrow took their unbeaten home run to 18 games and moved into second place in Division Three, probably the highest position they ever reached in the Football League. Diplomatically, they credited the goal to McLean.

Plymouth were left with a long, disconsolate journey home.

THE SOCCER WAR
MEXICO CITY, JUNE 1969

At stake was a place in the 1970 World Cup Finals. Two Latin American countries, Honduras and El Salvador, were to play off, home and away, and the winners would meet Haiti to contest one of 16 places available at Mexico's first World Cup Finals. The outcome of the Honduras–El Salvador confrontation was later dubbed the 'soccer war'.

Antagonism between Honduras and El Salvador had actually been smouldering for ten years or more. The countries had serious internal problems – over-population, poverty and dependence upon simple agricultural economies. By spring 1969 about 300,000 Salvadorans were living in the much larger bordering country of Honduras. Their presence began to be resented, and land-reform laws were introduced to deprive them of farms. On 30 April they were given 30 days to leave their land.

The mood can be gauged by some of the mud that was slung across the border in May. The Honduran Minister of Foreign Affairs linked Colgate toothpaste (made in El Salvador) to an increased incidence of cavities among Honduran children. El Salvador authorities alleged that Glostora haircream (made in Honduras) caused dandruff. By June, the month of the soccer games, tension was running exceedingly high.

Honduras were at home first. The Salvadorans stayed at the Hotel Prado in Tegucigalpa, where they were 'serenaded' all night by whistles, fireworks and shouting. The next day, in the bowl-like stadium at the base of a hill which sported a classical Peace Monument, El Salvador lost 1–0.

A week later came the return game in San Salvador. An El Salvador win would bring a play-off as the competition was on a points rather than goals basis. The Honduras players, not surprisingly, were treated to a reciprocal serenade the night before this return game. Many Hondurans who had travelled to San Salvador caught the hostile mood and decided to watch the game on television instead of attending the Flor Blanca stadium. When they witnessed the stone-throwing and water-bombing they must have been glad to have stayed at home. Furthermore, the game was one-sided. Two goals from Martinez (one a penalty) and one from Acevedo gave El Salvador a 3–0 lead at half-time. There was no second-half scoring but it was now one game each. A play-off was necessary.

Only two Honduran supporters were seriously injured but this was enough to cause outrage in local newspaper columns. The day after the game paramilitary groups in Honduras forcibly evicted Salvadoran peasants from lands they had farmed for years. Tens of thousands of Salvadorans flocked over the border, back to their already over-populated native country.

On 26 June El Salvador broke off diplomatic relations with Honduras. Three days later came the World Cup qualifying play-off. Fortunately, cool heads had suggested a neutral venue, the Aztec Stadium, Mexico City, and about 1,700 Mexican policemen were assigned to duty.

In the circumstances the game was surprisingly peaceful. True, there was one outburst of *'asesinos, asesinos'* ('murderers, murderers') from the El Salvador fans, but the fear of feuding among the crowd (about 15,000) proved unfounded, even when the game went into extra-time. The winning goal fell to El Salvador, who recorded a 3–2 victory. Martinez again scored twice.

Early in July Honduran and Salvadoran troops crossed the border. Honduras bragged it had the region's best air force, but, on 14 July, it was El Salvador who made a crucial aerial attack – on the airport at Tegucigalpa. This precipitated the so-called 'soccer war'. The war lasted four days, until economic sanctions by the Organization of American States (OAS) forced El Salvador to withdraw with a psychological victory. Those people who have studied the war, such as Thomas Anderson in *The War of the Dispossessed* and Robert Armstrong and Janet Shenk in *Salvador: The Face of Revolution*, have shown that it was caused by problematic relationships between peasants and landowners, soldiers and civilians, trade-unionists and employers, and was not over anything as 'trivial' as soccer. However, it was certainly one of the strangest political contexts in which a soccer game has occurred.

Nor was that all for the winners, whose progress towards the 1970 World Cup Finals continued to be very odd. After a sound 2–1 win in Haiti, El Salvador might have left reasonably confident. All they required was a draw at home. But Haiti brought along a witch-doctor. He sprinkled some powder on the field, chanted a spell and Haiti were three up at half-time. The two countries travelled to Kingston, Jamaica, for a closely contested play-off. The game's first goal didn't arrive until extra time, when Martinez scored for El Salvador. Then El Salvador's Argentinian coach Gregorio Bundio took one of the strangest tactical decisions of his career – he punched the witch-doctor and put him out of the game. El Salvador won 1–0.

Bundio had coached El Salvador through ten World Cup qualifying games (including two which went to extra-time), a war and the threat of a witch-doctor. However, he was dismissed from his job before the Mexico Finals, caught up in a dispute between the players and their government. The players felt they were owed money promised for reaching the Finals. The government said the money would have to go towards the costs of the war the players had helped to cause.

In Mexico, El Salvador lost three games – 3–0 to Belgium, 4–0 to Mexico and 2–0 to Russia. They held out for 44 minutes against the hosts, Mexico, and then a disputed goal provoked uproar, threatening to end the match. Eventually the Egyptian referee found an ideal solution – he blew for half-time – and the crowd were left to contemplate the chances of war in the second half.

SOUTH AMERICAN FREE-FOR-ALL

BUENOS AIRES, MARCH 1971

It happened in the closing minutes of a South American (Libertadores) Cup match. Argentinian champions Boca Juniors and Sporting Cristal of Peru were locked at two goals apiece, and 65,000 were watching the contest in Boca's Bombonera ('Chocolate Box') Stadium. Neither side had much chance to qualify from the four-team group, but when Ruben Zune, the Boca Juniors' captain, was tackled and toppled over, he saw red. First he saw his blood. Next he felt his own anger. He attacked his assailant, and then it started.

The scene was what United States ice-hockey followers would call a bench-emptying brawl. Officials, coaches, reserves and almost all the players joined in. Referee Alejandro Otero could do little on his own except stand and observe 19 players commit sending-off offences. He called in the police.

By the end of the fracas three players were injured. Zune's cut would need seven stitches. One Peruvian, Mellan, was carried from the field on a stretcher suffering from a fractured skull. Another, Campos, had a broken nose.

Three players – the two goalkeepers and Boca's Peruvian centre-half Menendez – had steered clear of the rumpus, but the other 19 were arrested by the police. The 16 uninjured players were taken to the police station and given a 30-day jail sentence.

There was real danger of the footballers sewing mailbags in shirts of different stripes with different numbers, but diplomats intervened swiftly. The sentences were suspended. Yet it was six weeks before all the Boca players had served their playing suspensions. Boca, the biggest club in Argentina, had reserves but not of the same standard.

This was another sad episode in the Libertadores Cup, the competition which feeds into the World Club Championship by pitting its winners against the European Cup holders. Originally the Champion Clubs Cup, it had already staged a 3½-hour marathon between Penarol and Santos in 1962 – the Chilean referee twice suspended the game when officials were hit by missiles from the crowd and there were allegations in 1966 that River Plate's two Uruguayans had sold the Argentinian club down its own river. Not to mention a 1970 Nacional–Penarol eruption which was almost on the same scale as the game which saw 19 players sent off. Almost, but not quite.

THE VITAL
DISPUTED GOAL
LEEDS, APRIL 1971

If soccer historians needed to choose one game as a watershed of soccer's modern era, then the Leeds–West Brom game of 1970–1 would be a strong candidate: winning was the sole objective for one team, the play was a hallmark of professionalism and gamesmanship, the referee's decisions were challenged, the crowd invaded the pitch and there was an early example of trial by television.

Don Revie's Leeds United were desperate to turn their success into more tangible honours. After winning the Second Division in 1964, they had won the League Championship once, the League Cup once and the Inter-Cities Fairs Cup once; but they also had a remarkable record of frustration – second in the League on three occasions, twice beaten FA Cup Finalists, twice beaten in FA Cup semi-finals, beaten by Celtic in a European Cup semi-final, beaten finalists in the Inter-Cities Fairs Cup and semi-finalists in another Fairs Cup year.

Now, as they raced neck and neck with Arsenal, came another excellent chance for the League Championship. Early exits from the League Cup and FA Cup – the latter an embarrassing defeat at Fourth Division Colchester United – left the League as Leeds' last hope of domestic success in 1970–1. They had four games to play. Their visitors on 17 April, West Bromwich Albion, were unlikely to stand in their way. West Brom hadn't won an away game for 16 months.

Nevertheless, West Brom were a better team than their poor League position and recent away results indicated. Centre-backs John Wile and John Kaye contained Leeds strikers Allan Clarke and Mick Jones with the help of offside tactics. Bobby Hope and the young Asa Hartford buzzed in midfield. And, after a mistake by Jack Charlton, Jeff Astle and Colin Suggett set up a fifteenth-minute goal for Tony Brown. At half-time West Brom led Leeds United 1–0.

According to Leeds supporters, the worst team on the pitch were the officials. They noted the name of referee Ray Tinkler, a company secretary from Lincolnshire, and linesman Colin Cartlich from Hull when they combined to rule Mick Jones offside when he put the ball into the West Brom net. Then, in the sixty-ninth minute, came the incident which pitched referee Tinkler into the national limelight.

Norman Hunter, Leeds' English international defender, played a careless pass. The ball bounced off Albion's Tony Brown and into space on the Leeds left flank. Brown took up the challenge and started a run for goal. His team-mate Colin Suggett was 10 yards (9.1m) further on, in a more central position, discreetly heading in the opposite direction to Brown ... but not discreetly enough. Suggett was spotted by linesman Troupe (South Shields), who raised his flag. Leeds midfielder Mick Bates appealed from the halfway-line. Tony Brown hesitated. Referee Tinkler raised his whistle towards his mouth, and then he thought again.

Consider the referee's position. There was no doubt that Suggett was in an offside position, but was he interfering with play or seeking to gain an advantage? Certainly the Leeds players thought he was, and that was enough to affect the play. Some people refused to accept the idea that a player might not be interfering with play, claiming that all players should be interfering with play throughout the game, for we were now on the verge of the concept of 'total football'. The law was clear. The referee had discretion to decide.

Confusion was caused by the linesman's role. His raised flag was informing the tall, balding Tinkler that a player was in an offside position. The referee would decide if the player was interfering with play. But some referees also asked the linesmen to decide before raising their flags.

Referee Ray Tinkler waved play on. Tony Brown continued his run, homing in on the near post. Brown passed the ball in front of Gary Sprake's goal. It was tapped into the net by Jeff Astle, who might have been offside but the linesman wasn't in the best position to see. Tinkler gave a goal.

The entire Leeds team surrounded the referee. About 20 spectators ran on to the field and police closed them down. Players protected the referee, but the linesman at the other end, Colin Cartlich, was hit by a can and needed treatment from Leeds trainer Les Cocker.

It was some time before order was restored and the game resumed. Albion now led 2–0, and Leeds' Championship hopes were receding. Although Allan Clarke pulled back a goal, Leeds lost 2–1. Sixteen days later Arsenal won the Championship by a point.

The outcry from Leeds officials after the game was as provocative as that of the spectators. Manager Don Revie called for full-time referees and said that nine months' work had been ruined by one man (meaning Tinkler). Chairman Percy Woodward was even more outspoken, almost supporting the actions of the pitch invaders. Leeds United were later fined £750 and Elland Road was closed for the first four home matches of the next season.

These events may not seem strange by today's standards. But at the time they certainly were. Yet it was only soccer history's curious knack of repeating itself. Back in 1912 West Brom had won 1–0 at Leeds City in an FA Cup tie, and Leeds supporters greeted the only goal with claims of handball, offside and that the ball went through a hole in the net. Leeds manager Scott Walford had to plead with hundreds of spectators before they went home.

THE HIGH-SCORERS'
CUP FINAL

WEST BROMWICH, AUGUST 1971

The Watney Cup, an early sponsored tournament, was designed for high-scoring teams, not that there were many about in the early 1970s. West Brom (68 goals scored in the First Division in 1970–1) and Colchester United (70 goals in Division Four) were among the qualifiers. Their Watney Cup Final, played at the end of the eight-team pre-season tournament, justified their selection. Under an experimental offside law, the game had plenty of goals, a penalty-kick competition and an unusual result.

Don Howe had just taken over as West Brom manager. A former West Brom, Arsenal and England player, he was fresh from success as coach to the Arsenal double-winning team. People were predicting a stronger defence than under previous manager Alan Ashman.

Colchester United manager Dick Graham also had West Brom connections – he had been trainer and coach under Vic Buckingham – but had enjoyed a less illustrious playing career than Howe, as a goalkeeper with Leicester City, Northampton Town and Crystal Palace. As a manager he was one of the original gimmick men, shuffling players' shirts at Crystal Palace – the centre-half will wear number seven, and so on – and turning the dressing-room into a relaxing lounge. At Colchester he produced a super-fit team and promised to scale the walls of Colchester Castle if they beat Leeds United in the FA Cup. They won 3–2.

An experimental offside law meant players could only be offside inside the penalty area. At half-time West Brom led 3–2 with goals by Len Cantello, Jeff Astle and Colin Suggett. Mick Mahon and David Simmons scored for Colchester.

Mahon equalised in the sixty-fifth minute and Colchester looked to have won the game when Brian Lewis scored an eighty-eighth-minute penalty. But Astle equalised: 4–4.

The game went to penalty-kicks. West Brom shot first. They scored three out of the first four and needed the fifth to stay in the game as Colchester had scored their first four. Len Cantello shot over the crossbar and Fourth Division Colchester won with a penalty in hand.

THE ENDLESS CUP TIE
ALVECHURCH, OXFORD AND
BIRMINGHAM, NOVEMBER 1971

When Alvechurch of the Midland Combination and Oxford City of the Isthmian League played out their final qualifying round FA Cup tie, people began to joke that the Cup Final might have to be delayed. It took six games and 660 playing minutes to decide the tie. Finally, Bobby Hope's 588th-minute headed goal divided the teams and champagne flowed in both dressing-rooms.

The marathon started and finished on treacherous pitches. The Cup tie moved from Alvechurch's Lye Meadow (with its corner-to-corner slope) to Aston Villa's Villa Park, calling on the way at Oxford City's White House, Birmingham City's St Andrews and Oxford United's Manor Stadium (where two games were played).

At Alvechurch, the home team led 2–0 but Oxford clawed back into the game to force the first draw. Had Oxford City goalkeeper Peter Harris not dived bravely at the feet of Bobby Hope (not the Scottish international) late in the game, a lot of travelling might have been avoided.

The Cup tie was chronicled excellently by *Oxford Mail* reporter Jim Rosenthal, who covered five of the six games. His only mistake was to suggest that Alvechurch might have missed their best chance. 'In this competition,' Rosenthal wrote, 'you only get one bite at the cherry, and Oxford will want to emphasise that point at the White House tomorrow night.'

In fact, Alvechurch had another five bites at the cherry, something neither Rosenthal nor anyone else could have predicted. By the time of the first replay, the two teams knew the winners would play Aldershot (away) in the first round of the FA Cup proper. Aldershot manager Jimmy Melia turned up to watch his future opponents without realising that he would have four more opportunities to see them play. By the end of the saga Melia might have considered how best to use his time.

The first replay, the most rugged of the six games, had two first-half goals, shared of course. By the end of extra-time the two teams were exhausted, but Alvechurch maintained their season's unbeaten away record.

The next game was in Birmingham – almost a home game for Alvechurch – and the 3,600 crowd was the highest attendance of the six. Having drawn a league game on the Saturday, Oxford City extended their sequence with an equaliser just after half-time of this second replay. But that was the last goal the Cup tie produced for about 330 minutes. There was enough action. Another fine save from Harris (after 324 minutes) kept the third match alive, while City's Andy Mitchell cleared from the goal-line (365 minutes) and Tommy Eales twice hit the crossbar (388 minutes and 449 minutes) in the goalless fourth game.

It became an endurance test. Alvechurch midfielder Derek Davis, a car-worker on nights, had to be rested from the fourth game. City's Eric Metcalfe, a schoolteacher, received a hairline fibula fracture in the fifth game. The trainers became experts on cramp.

The *Oxford Mail's* Bill Beckett, deputising for Jim Rosenthal at the fourth game, reported that someone in the crowd suggested an annual reunion for those who had thus far watched all four games. Unfortunately, a few minutes after the fifth game (one of three in Oxford), an elderly Alvechurch supporter collapsed and died.

By the sixth game, at Villa Park, there was little new

for coaches John Fisher (Oxford City) and Rhys Davies (Alvechurch) to try. The two teams knew each other very well. Fisher was forced to make changes, however, as the Army couldn't release two of his men and two other key players were injured. Then came Bobby Hope's goal in the eighteenth minute of the sixth game. The winners were Alvechurch.

For the record, the six games were as follows: Sat. 6 Nov. (Alvechurch) Alvechurch 2 (Horne, Allner), Oxford City 2 (McCrae, Metcalfe); Tues. 9 Nov. (Oxford) Oxford City 1 (Eales), Alvechurch 1 (Allner); Mon. 15 Nov. (Birmingham) Alvechurch 1 (Alner), Oxford City 1 (Goucher); Wed. 17 Nov. (Oxford) Alvechurch 0, Oxford City 0; Sat. 20 Nov. (Oxford) Alvechurch 0, Oxford City 0; Mon. 22 Nov. (Villa Park) Alvechurch 1 (Hope), Oxford City 0. (All except the first and last went to extra-time.)

The first–round game against Aldershot was delayed, but only by four days. Alvechurch, playing their ninth game in 18 days, went down 4–2 and were out of the competition.

When the draw for the FA Amateur Cup was made a week later you can almost imagine a wag going into the Oxford City dressing-room: 'Heard the draw, lads? Alvechurch away.' Fortunately, it didn't happen.

'We didn't know the Oxford players at the start but we were on first-name terms at the end,' says Graham Alner who played for Alvechurch in all six matches. 'We were turning up as if long-lost mates – the same teams, the same players, the same result. It was a big experience for me. It was character hardening. Tactics went out of the window. We just carried on playing the same way. Before every game, Rhys Davis used to say, "Go out and give it some tonk and bottle." That was his favourite phrase at the time.'

REFEREE WHO FORGOT THE RULES

LISBON, NOVEMBER 1971

One of the most embarrassing refereeing errors of recent years came when Dutchman van Ravens got the rules wrong in the second leg of a second-round European Cup-winners' Cup tie between Sporting Lisbon and Glasgow Rangers.

All referees make mistakes occasionally. Such errors usually result from the officials' inability to see everything from every angle and make the correct split-second decision. This gives rise to a spate of jokes and stories about 'blindness' ('I agreed to escort the referee to the railway station,' said the policeman, 'because I always like to take care of the handicapped') and 'bias' ('We were playing against 12 men'). Those familiar with refereeing history are probably aware that many contemporary referees are often compared with the much-respected official in the 1878 FA Cup Final, Mr Segar Bastard.

Most major refereeing howlers occurred in the early days of soccer. There was the referee who ordered off a dumb man for abusive language (the decision was later reversed), the referee who headed a goal (he apologised but had to let the goal stand) and the referee who stood in a dressing-room washbowl and broke it.

In the post-war era a referee at Sunderland in 1954 started the second half before realising that only one linesman was in place. In front of 43,000 people, his face was as red as the missing flag.

At Wimbledon, in 1983, a referee wrongly awarded Millwall a goal after Wimbledon full-back Wally Downes chipped a direct free-kick over goalkeeper Dave Beasant's head and into his own net. The correct decision here is a corner-kick; the early rule-makers sensibly decided that a team scoring in its own net from a direct free-kick shouldn't be punished more heavily than if it had done so from an indirect free-kick, as the offence being punished was obviously more serious in the first instance.

Refereeing can give rise to all manner of wild questions about soccer oddities and offbeat features of the game. For example, a penalty kick is taken, the ball bursts as it is kicked, the casing flies over the crossbar, the lace spins out and wraps itself around the goalkeeper's neck, hindering him from saving the bladder as it sails into the net – what is the correct decision?

That incident, as far as I am aware, never happened, even in the days when balls had laces. But the events in Lisbon in 1971 showed that one referee had not been tested on the rules of the competition.

Rangers had won the first leg at Ibrox Park 3–2, after being 2–0 ahead at one stage. Now they had a difficult game in Lisbon. Sporting Lisbon twice took the lead. Each time Colin Stein equalised. Then Rangers' Scottish international centre-half Ron McKinnon fractured a leg, and Sporting took the lead again with 25 minutes to play. Somehow Rangers hung on to take the tie into extra-time.

During this period both teams scored once. Thereupon, referee van Ravens ordered each team to take five penalties to decide the tie. Rangers qualified for some sort of record by missing all five kicks. In fact, Tommy McLean missed twice as the Sporting goalkeeper moved too quickly for the first. Sporting won 3–0 on penalties and were through to the next round. Or were they?

The Scottish journalists were already scratching their heads in bewilderment. Surely, they thought, away goals count double in the event of a tie. At the end of extra-time Rangers had scored three away goals against Sporting's two in Glasgow.

The referee was wrong. Rangers were indeed the winners. The UEFA officials later reversed the referee's decision and suspended the Dutch referee. The rules were very clear. The provision that away goals counted double in the event of a draw also applied to those scored in extra-time. That gave rise to an even better sporting question: which team missed all its six penalties during a penalty shoot-out and still won the tie?

That season Glasgow Rangers won the European Cup-winners' Cup.

SIXTEEN MINUTES OF DISBELIEF

BIRKENHEAD, MARCH 1972

A strange match creates a crowd atmosphere, a prevailing group mood of anger, laughter, shock or sheer bewilderment, depending on the events concerned. Sometimes, when a match gaily runs completely out of control, spectators turn to neighbours for confirmation of what they are seeing.

That happened to me the night Tranmere Rovers played Walsall. I experienced 16 minutes of disbelief.

It was my second season of supporting Rovers. I had cheered them through their glorious record-breaking season of 1970–1 – no team had ever drawn as many as 22 League games before – and now watched in awe as they blazed a trail towards the Division Three relegation zone. Most Rovers home games were on Friday evenings in those days, the crowd swollen by Liverpool or Everton fans taking a night off from the Anfield Kop or Gladys Street end.

Liverpool fans were particularly enticed in 1971–2, when Tranmere signed Liverpool internationals Ron 'Rowdy' Yeats, soon to become Rovers' manager, and Tommy Lawrence, a goalkeeper affectionately known by the Kop as the 'Fat Cat' or 'Flying Pig'. Lawrence was a roly-poly goalie, small and podgy, deceptively agile, fearless and cumbersome enough to make it very awkward for forwards when he narrowed their shooting angles.

By the time he joined Tranmere, Lawrence was well past his Scottish international peak, slower and heavier, and looking even less like an athlete. I remember one incident when he waddled and grovelled endlessly along the goal-line to collect a stray back-pass near the corner of his penalty area. With no one remotely near him, he stopped the ball with his body, knocked it out of the penalty area, trod on it, picked himself up, dragged the ball back into the penalty area and stood, eventually, clutching his treasure. The crowd had been deathly quiet. Then one spectator spoke clearly and loudly in unsolicited admiration. 'All I saw was a green blur,' he said.

By the end of March 1972, Rovers were still drawing games but not crowds. 'If they played in our back yard I'd draw the curtains,' I remember someone saying at the end of one game. There were just 2,320 present the Monday night Walsall visited.

Occupants of the press-box must have been grateful when news of the attendance reached them in the second half. They could add a comment on Rovers' lowest attendance of the season – in fact it was one of the five lowest in the Division that season – to the meagre notes they already had: drab and goalless ... both sides failed to control the ball in the wind ... Tranmere's slump continued ... Rovers badly missed injured assistant manager Ron Yeats ... no sign of a goal ... Chic Brodie showed some neat touches in midfield ... Rovers failed to take advantage of the gale at their backs in the first half ... after 62 minutes Adrian Maher came on as substitute for ex-Walsall centre-forward John Manning ... neither goalkeeper had a save to make ...

I entertained myself by walking around the terraces, until I was behind Tommy Lawrence's goal, totally alone in that section of the ground. A bitter, biting wind tore through my clothing. In front of me, Lawrence stalked his penalty area to keep warm. I thought about the 20,000 Anfield Kop. Here, at Prenton Park, I was on my own, and it was too cold to stay.

I was on my way home, having just reached the Shed, when the game woke up and went crazy.

A free-kick to Walsall and Mick Evans thunders it noisily against the post and Walsall come again, Chris Jones to Bobby Shinton, whose shot wiggles in the wind with Tommy Lawrence wondering where it went and the game's been given a goal, so Rovers must attack, which they do, Trevor Storton shooting and Stan Jones deflecting the ball up and over Bob Wesson for an own-goal equaliser, and now the action's back to Tommy Lawrence who knocks down Colin Harrison's shot for Geoff Morris to score another for Walsall and there's nobody on the 'Kop' to see it from close quarters, or to strain their eyes as Wesson makes a great save at the other end and another and another but he can't reach Storton's cross and Maher scores another equaliser so Walsall come straight down and Bobby Shinton topples over Syd Farrimond's legs and Harrison hits the penalty past Lawrence for the third Walsall goal and Rovers have hardly any time left when Maher puts over a corner-kick and Storton lunges and it's Rovers' third equaliser in about ten minutes and the game ends and we can breathe again.

Three-three in 16 minutes. Had it been like that all through the game it would have finished 17 apiece. I have seen games lurch out of control on many other occasions, but never to that extent and never after 74 minutes of tedium. Football, at times, thoroughly rewards the patience of people at places like Prenton Park. That season Tranmere Rovers escaped relegation on goal average.

CROWD POWER

NEWCASTLE, MARCH 1974

Should the Newcastle United–Nottingham Forest FA Cup tie have been abandoned after 55 minutes and the result allowed to stand? If so, Forest would have won 3–1 and gained a place in the semi-final. Instead it took five hours of playing time and many more hours spent in meetings before the outcome was settled. The eventual winners were Newcastle United.

On form, Second Division Forest were given little chance against First Division United, but St James's Park was a likely place for an FA Cup upset. That season Newcastle had twice been held to shock home draws – by non-League Hendon and Fourth Division Scunthorpe United – while two years earlier non-League Hereford United had done the same and then beaten Newcastle at Edgar Street.

Goals by Ian Bowyer and Liam O'Kane gave Forest a 2–1 lead at half-time. Then the eruption came in the fifty-fifth minute. David Craig fouled Duncan McKenzie and referee Gordon Kew gave Forest a penalty-kick. Newcastle centre-half Pat Howard argued so much that he was sent off. George Lyall scored the penalty and United, trailing 3–1 on goals and 11–10 down on men, looked a doomed side. A small section of the crowd changed all that.

According to police estimates, between 300 and 500 spectators took part in the pitch invasion. They spilled on to the pitch and charged. Two Forest players were assaulted, so the referee took the players to the dressing-rooms for safety.

Twenty-three people were taken to hospital and 103 others treated on the ground. The police made 39 arrests and took eight minutes to clear the pitch.

The teams returned and the game continued, but Forest had lost their initiative. Newcastle surged forward with the bulk of the 54,000 crowd in support. Intimidated, Forest conceded three goals in the last 20 minutes – a penalty by Terry McDermott, a flying header by John Tudor and a volley by Bobby Moncur. One neutral observer said he thought Moncur looked offside but with the crowd in that mood the linesman dared not raise his flag – he would have been lynched.

A special FA commission concluded that the 4–3 Newcastle victory was achieved in a hostile environment. Even though Newcastle had already been drawn against Burnley in the semi-final, the result of their sixth-round game was annulled. The FA ordered the match to be replayed on neutral ground, a decision which infuriated Newcastle officials and players. 'My reaction is one of disgust, but not surprise,' said centre-forward Malcolm MacDonald. 'I half-expected a ridiculous solution, and they came up with one.'

It took two games to reach a decision. The teams drew 0–0 (after extra-time) at Goodison Park on Monday 18 March, and, three days later, at the same venue, Malcolm MacDonald scored the only goal of the game. That season Newcastle reached the FA Cup Final, losing to Liverpool, while people pondered on the long-term implications of that March day at St James's Park. If a partisan crowd was worth a goal start, then a pitch invasion could be worth three.

UNDER THE SPELL
LONDON, APRIL 1975

I well remember a Saturday in the 1970s when I turned up to watch New Brighton lose a Cheshire League game. New Brighton, losing consistently at the time, were playing the top of the league. Imagine how stunned I was when the Rakers – our affectionate term for the New Brighton lads – went delirious with energy and scored three times in the first half-hour. 'There's been annippnotist in dressing-room,' I was informed by a nearby spectator, who obviously saw how pale I looked. But New Brighton's major tactical defect, I discovered later, was not to call in the hypnotist at half-time. A tired New Brighton team played a more predictable second half and were pegged back to 3–3.

In recent times, hypnotists have become more accepted as a means to relax players and inspire confidence. Ronald Markham, who was known as Romark on the stage, worked with Millwall when they were promoted to Division Two in 1976, and with Halifax Town when, as a Fourth Division team in 1980, they beat First Division Manchester City 1–0 in the FA Cup.

One particular match worth featuring was Tottenham Hotspur's contest with Leeds United at the end of the 1974–5 First Division season. A Spurs defeat would mean relegation to the Second Division. Terry Neill, Spurs' manager, called in Ronald Markham, who hypnotised the team before the game, concentrating on three players –

Alfie Conn, Cyril Knowles and Martin Chivers, who was back in the first team after an absence of two months.

Cyril Knowles had been suffering with a knee injury for more than a year. Markham asked him to talk through a goal he had once scored from a free-kick. The response, during the game, was almost instantaneous. Inside a few minutes Spurs had a free-kick just outside the penalty area. Knowles took it and scored.

Chivers scored a second for Tottenham in the fiftieth minute, and Knowles, playing full-back, made it three from a penalty. Although Jordan scored for Leeds, Conn made it 4–1 in the seventy-fifth minute. The final score was 4–2 and Spurs stayed in the First Division for another two seasons.

THE 28-PENALTY SHOOT-OUT

HONG KONG, JUNE 1975

The Asia Cup semi-final between North Korea and Hong Kong finished 2–2 after 90 minutes and 3–3 after extra-time. The ensuing penalty shoot-out had spectators wondering whether it might have been quicker to play another game.

It was an agonising few hours for North Korea coach Pak Du-ik, best remembered in Britain for the goal that beat Italy in the 1966 World Cup Finals. His team led by two goals in the game against Hong Kong, then looked in danger of losing 3–2 when Hong Kong scored with seven minutes of extra-time remaining. The penalty shoot-out tested the coach's nerve even more.

Hong Kong took the first penalty and scored. North Korea took the second penalty and scored. Hong Kong took the next and missed. North Korea missed their second too, and then the neck-and-neck competition continued.

Each team scored five of their first six. Lai Sun-cheung took Hong Kong's seventh kick. He missed. It was now 'sudden death'. Up stepped Cha Jung-sok to take North Korea's seventh kick. Hong Kong goalkeeper Chu Kwok-kuen saved it.

It was back to stalemate, each team scoring with alternate kicks. Soon, all the players except the goalkeepers had taken kicks, and they had to start over again.

Wu Kwok-hung took Hong Kong's thirteenth kick and missed. Pak Jung-hun had the chance to win the game for

North Korea but his penalty was saved by Chu Kwok-kuen. The duel continued.

Hong Kong missed their fourteenth penalty too, so Kim Jungmm was the next potential match-winner for North Korea. He shot left-footed, low to the goalkeeper's right. Chu Kwok-kuen moved the wrong way and the game was over. North Korea had won the penalty shoot-out 11–10 on the twenty-eighth penalty. They were very tired when they beat China in the Asia Cup Final a few days later.

OVATION FOR A STREAKER

PETERBOROUGH, AUGUST 1975

She waited until half-time on the first day of the new season, a day warm enough for what she intended. The teams returned from their break and walked, or trotted, to their places, the players in little huddles, discussing the half-time words of their managers, Noel Cantwell (Peterborough United) and Doug Fraser (Walsall). Then came a distraction.

The teenager with waist-length hair was clad, while on the terraces, in a light-coloured blouse and dark, bell-bottomed trousers. As she ran on to the London Road pitch she peeled off her blouse and undid her bra. The crowd cheered. Not the usual excited cheer for egging on the team during the game – just a light-hearted, good-humoured cheer.

Naked to the waist, she ran around in circles among the players and then set off back towards the terrace. A policeman met her there. He took off his helmet, covered up her bare breasts and led her gently out of the ground. All the crowd shouted good-humoured comments. I won't speculate as to what they were, but the *Peterborough Evening Telegraph*, on the Monday after the game (which finished 0–0), ran a front-page cartoon showing two supporters talking: 'A good afternoon's entertainment, Albert … Posh got a point and the streaker had two.'

Yes, there was also a game. Both teams had new signings on show – Miah Dennehy for Walsall and Peter Eustace for Peterborough – and the two goalkeepers, Mick Kearns (Walsall) and Eric Steele (Peterborough), both played well. The dearth of goals gave the papers the chance to say that the streaker earned the biggest cheer of the afternoon, but that was probably stretching the point.

There was also a streaker at Arsenal in 1982, but, so far, no soccer streaker has achieved the prominence of Erika Roe, who, when 24, ran semi-naked on to the Twickenham pitch at half-time of an England–Australia rugby international. Roe chose London rather than London Road, Peterborough, a televised game rather than a Third Division soccer match, a capacity crowd rather than an attendance of 7,174 people. Film of Erika streaking was shown on television news and she was soon offered a job modelling double-breasted jackets.

THE ONE-SCORER
FOUR-GOAL DRAW
LEICESTER, MARCH 1976

Northern Ireland international Chris Nicholl, later manager of Southampton, played 648 Football League games during his long career with Halifax Town, Luton Town, Aston Villa, Southampton and Grimsby Town. None was more bizarre than Aston Villa's away game at Leicester City in March 1976, which goes down in history for Nicholl's remarkable piece of goalscoring. The tall central defender scored all four goals in a 2–2 draw. Twice he headed own-goals to put Leicester ahead. Twice he equalised with close-range shots.

The game at Leicester was the eighteenth of 21 away games Aston Villa failed to win that season, their first season back in Division One. They started well enough, but Leicester went ahead after 15 minutes, Nicholl heading Brian Alderson's shot on to a better course for it to find the net. In the fortieth minute, however, after Brian Little's header had created confusion in the Leicester penalty area, Nicholl hooked in an equaliser for Villa.

Eight minutes after half-time Chris Nicholl conceded his second own-goal. Leicester's Frank Worthington lobbed the ball into the penalty area and Nicholl, challenging with Bob Lee, sent another fine header past John Burridge. But, once again, he cancelled out his own-goal with one at the other end. Four minutes were left when 'Chico' Hamilton sent over a corner-kick. A scramble in the goalmouth gave

Nicholl a chance to put boot on ball, and there was his fourth goal of the game, his second for Villa.

Chris Nicholl's amazing feat of two for each side equalled the 'achievement' of Sam Wynne in a 1923 game for Oldham Athletic against Manchester United. Wynne scored a free-kick and a penalty-kick for Oldham and two own-goals for Manchester United. Oldham won 3–2. But, in Nicholl's case, all his goals came from open play and they were the only goals of the game.

Also, there were a couple of strange indicators from the previous week. Chris Nicholl had scored an own-goal a week before, diverting a shot from Tottenham Hotspur's Ralph Coates past John Burridge. And, on the same day, Leicester had beaten Middlesbrough, the only goal of the game being an own-goal by tall Middlesbrough central defender Stuart Boam.

One of the strangest things about Nicholl's performance was his two goals for Villa. His goals usually came from his head, but here he was scoring with his feet. It was surprising that Villa never used him as an out-and-out attacker. After all, that day at Leicester he demonstrated that he had the one thing that all natural goalscorers possess – a beautiful sense of balance.

THE GAME THAT NEVER WAS

LEATHERHEAD, FEBRUARY 1978

Leatherhead were drawn at home to Dartford in the second round of the FA Trophy. Conditions were not good, but match referee Vickers of Essex declared the pitch fit after an inspection an hour and a half before kick-off. Dartford never turned up.

The Leatherhead players waited, the crowd at Fetcham Grove waited, even the Dartford directors who had travelled under their own steam waited. There was no sign of the Dartford team coach.

There were four differing accounts of why the Dartford coach-driver was told to turn round at Croydon, which was over halfway of a journey of less than 30 miles (48.3km). Certainly someone made a telephone call from Croydon. One account says a young girl answered and told them the game was postponed. Another says it was the secretary who confirmed the match was off. A third account suggests Dartford were the victims of a hoax. A fourth guess might be that someone dialled the wrong number. If a stranger phoned your house at Saturday lunchtime and came straight to the point – 'Is the game on, Leatherhead?' – you probably wouldn't be stuck for a negative answer.

So, while Dartford players were at home watching the rugby on television, Leatherhead players were put through a stiff training session. Although people at the ground felt Dartford were to blame, no one was fined over the incident.

Dartford were allowed to replay the fixture without punishment. On the following Thursday Leatherhead won 5–1, Chris Kelly scoring two goals.

The morals of the tale are to ensure that telephones are staffed responsibly at key times and to seek confirmation of any news received. These points can be made more forcibly by reference to a cunning piece of corruption which took place in 1904. Before an important game between Bristol East and Warmley, the Bristol East goalkeeper received a telegram from the Bristol East secretary saying the match would not take place. Warmley were delighted when Bristol East were forced to scratch around at the last minute for a replacement goalkeeper. When it was later learned that the telegram had been sent by Warmley officials, the Football Association handed out three suspensions.

WARRING TEAM-MATES
LONDON, JANUARY 1979

There is a clear statement contained in the twelfth of soccer's 17 laws: a player shall be sent off the field of play if, in the opinion of the referee, he is guilty of violent conduct or serious foul play.

This statement does not specify that the violent conduct must be towards an opponent for it to warrant a sending-off punishment. The violence could be directed at a team-mate, although that is extremely rare.

There were five minutes to play in the game at the Valley Stadium. Charlton Athletic and Maidstone United were drawing 1–1 in their FA Cup third-round game. Mike Flanagan, scorer of Charlton's equaliser a few minutes before, played the ball through. Derek Hales, Flanagan's co-striker, was given offside. The bearded Hales was not pleased.

Hales made it clear that he wanted the ball played earlier. Flanagan said something to the effect that he had been doing that all season and it hadn't come to much. Hales and Flanagan swore at each other. Then they started fighting. Referee Brian Martin had no option but to send off both players.

Everyone was stunned. It was outside most people's experience. There had been a similar incident in Scotland, when two Stranraer players came to blows in 1975, but they had escaped with cautions and very few heard about it. Now

Charlton had to complete the game with nine men. They held on and won a replay.

The following week over 10,000 spectators attended the replay in the hope of seeing an upset. The Southern League Premier Division team, unbeaten in 14 games, now had ground advantage, and Second Division Charlton would be without Hales and Flanagan, suspended after their sending-off incident. What they saw was a match which was definitely a bit strange.

Goals by David Campbell and Martyn Robinson gave Charlton a healthy 2–0 lead. Glen Coupland pulled one back with four minutes to play. Then the floodlights went out.

The lights had overheated. There was a 17-minute time-out before they were restored and play resumed. The final two or three minutes were played out with no more score. Maidstone, who had beaten Exeter City in the previous round, were knocked out of the FA Cup for that season. Charlton went out at Bristol Rovers in the fourth round, the only game Mike Flanagan played during the last four months of the season.

Hales and Flanagan both received punishments from Charlton, and Flanagan was later suspended by the club when he implied that the personal difficulties with Hales would prevent him playing. Six months later, after much inactivity, Flanagan moved to Crystal Palace. From there he moved to Queen's Park Rangers. In January 1984, however, Flanagan signed once more for Charlton Athletic, where for nearly a year he resumed his successful striking partnership with Derek Hales.

THE FALKLAND ISLANDS GAMES

SOUTH GEORGIA, THROUGH THE 1970s

Sometimes the setting is enough to provide a strange game. In 1920–1, at Fishguard on the Welsh coast, players had to swim out to sea to rescue a football before a game could continue. Other games are played next to rivers, with trees overhanging the pitch or with quarries behind one goal. All seem odd when encountered for the first time.

In the 1970s, the British Antarctic Survey team regularly played soccer matches against the crews of ships using the water facilities of the whaling station on South Georgia in the Falkland Isles. Their team was selected from about 20 men on base. They changed in an old cinema and drove to the whaling-station pitch in a tractor and trailer. The pitch, like all unusual settings, was worth a start in goals to the home team. It was cut into the base of a mountain, and local grass covered the stone surface, which, obviously, wasn't the best surface for sliding tackles or the longevity of football boots and footballs. There were no pitch markings but natural boundaries. Three sides were marked by obvious banks. The fourth fell away so that the ball could roll into a stream, a dyke or down drainage holes. Mount Hodges (2,000ft/610m) acted as a huge spion kop.

A LEGAL PRECEDENT
LEAMINGTON SPA, JANUARY 1980

A foul tackle by Gurdever Basi of Khalsa Football Club broke the right leg of James Condon of Whittle Wanderers in a local league game. Condon was off work for nine months. More than a year after the game he issued a writ suing Basi for damages. He alleged negligence and deliberate and wrongful assault. He won his case.

The case was heard by Judge Wootton at Warwick County Court in March 1984. Basi was found guilty of negligence and Condon was awarded damages of £4,900 plus interest and costs. Basi's appeal was dismissed by Judge Donaldson in May 1985.

For a description of the incident we can rely on the referee's report of the Whittle Wanderers–Khalsa game. An experienced Class 1 official, he wrote this: 'After 62 minutes of play of the above game, a player from Whittle Wanderers received possession of the ball some 15 yards [13.7m] inside Khalsa Football Club's half of the field of play. This Whittle Wanderers player, upon realising that he was about to be challenged for the ball by an opponent, pushed the ball away. As he did so, the opponent (the defendant) challenged, by sliding in from a distance of 3–4 yards [2.7–3.7m]. The slide tackle came late, and was made in a reckless and dangerous manner, by lunging with his boot studs showing about 12–18in [30.5–45.7cm] from the ground. The result of this tackle was that (the plaintiff) sustained a broken right leg. In my opinion, the tackle constituted serious foul play and I sent (the defendant) from the field of play.'

Such cases depend on determining what is meant by 'care'. Footballers have a duty to take all reasonable care, bearing in mind the circumstances in which they are placed. In this case Basi was guilty of serious and dangerous foul play which showed a reckless disregard of the plaintiff's safety and fell far below standards which might reasonably be expected in anyone pursuing the game.

So, if you are a player, take care.

THE 'ESCAPE TO VICTORY' GAME

HUNGARY, JUNE–AUGUST 1980

John Huston's remake of the Hungarian film *The Last Goal*, released as *Escape to Victory* in Britain and *Victory* in the United States, was not well received by the critics. The film was more memorable for its soccer sequence than for its portrayal of the realism of war. (If only one could say that about all soccer games.)

Huston's film was set in the Second World War. The match revolves around the idea that nations can settle their differences on the soccer field. A German commandant challenges a team of prisoners to a game against their German guards. Captain Colby, played by Michael Caine, organises the prisoner-of-war team, which contains some very familiar faces. The actors are experienced professional footballers, like Brazilian Pelé, Argentinian Ossie Ardiles, former England captain Bobby Moore and Scotland international John Wark. The team's goalkeeper, played by Sylvester Stallone, is more obviously a novice. During filming Stallone discovered that soccer was a very tough sport. Flinging himself around like an acrobat, Stallone broke a finger, damaged his knees and bruised other fingers. When he returned to the United States he described himself as a walking blood clot.

And so, to the climax of the film – the soccer game.

The Germans, to ensure a propaganda victory, have engaged the services of a supportive referee. At half-time the Germans have a 2–0 lead. Then comes a difficult decision for the prisoners. A tunnel has been dug to take them from their dressing-room to safety, but they also want to stay and see through the game – they feel they can win.

Sure enough, they continue the game rather than escape. They pull back the two goals and Stallone saves a penalty. The crowd invades the pitch and the team escape in the confusion.

Escape to Victory was not the first soccer film. The earliest talking picture to include soccer scenes was probably *The Great Game*, which staged a game at Barnes and included in its cast Jack Cock, an England international who was playing for Millwall at the time (1930). Later in the 1930s, the *Arsenal Stadium Mystery* was filmed from Leonard Gribble's book, and a few soccer sequences were set up to portray the fictitious crack amateur team called the Trojans. More recently, Sweden has produced *Stubby*, the United States has given the world *Boys in Company C* and *The Longest Yard*, while Britain chipped in with *Yesterday's Hero* and *Gregory's Girl*, the latter almost certainly being the pick of the lot, and *Bend It Like Beckham*.

Escape to Victory shows how a soccer game can be staged and filmed to suit an audience's fantasy or the director's concept of an unlikely encounter. There is, however, an element of truth in it. Soccer was indeed played in certain prison camps.

BEHIND CLOSED DOORS

WEST HAM, OCTOBER 1980

The sound of boot on ball echoed around the ground, and the only other noise came from players shouting for the ball and club officials yelling from the sidelines. Such a scene is very familiar in amateur soccer, but this was a vital European Cup-winners' Cup tie between West Ham United and Castilla of Spain. Five hundred police ringed Upton Park to ensure that the game was played behind closed doors. This was West Ham's punishment following crowd trouble during the first leg of the first-round Cup tie in Spain.

West Ham lost the first leg 3–1 despite leading through David Cross's goal at half-time. Second-half problems included not only the faulty back-passes by Bonds and Pike, which led to Castilla goals, but also the need for the Spanish police to intervene on the terraces. Fifty West Ham supporters were ejected from the Spanish stadium and one was killed by a bus after the game.

Initially, West Ham were fined £7,750 and ordered to play their next two home European matches at least 186 miles (300km) from London. Some were arguing that this was a fairly lenient sentence – Rangers, Leeds United and Manchester United had all received European bans after crowd trouble abroad – but when West Ham appealed and presented evidence of the precautions taken, the fine was quashed and the ban on 'away' home matches lifted.

Sunderland's offer of a ground wouldn't be needed; West Ham were told to play behind closed doors.

Each club was allowed a 70-man delegation (including players). There were journalists present, and 16 ball-boys were recruited to retrieve the ball from the empty terraces. An attendance of 262 was recorded. Receipts were nil.

For once, the shouts from West Ham officials on the bench – John Lyall, Mick McGiven and Eddie Baily – could be heard clearly by the players (and probably by the police outside). The Spanish radio commentator, too, could be heard chattering to the people back home. The shouts of the players were audibly English and Spanish.

West Ham scored three times in the first half. There was no roar from the crowd, no response to indicate a goal to those inside and outside. David Cross found himself looking at the referee to check whether he had really scored.

Castilla scored and took the game to extra-time. In the empty, eerie stadium Cross scored two more and West Ham took control. They had lost revenue but won the match. After 120 minutes' play, the fortunate few went out to tell the world what had happened.

THE BROKEN GOALPOST
CHESTER, SEPTEMBER 1981

Plymouth Argyle's David Kemp headed the ball towards goal. Chester goalkeeper Grenville Millington stretched to make the save. He knocked the ball away and collided with an upright. The goalpost snapped near its base, the crossbar swung freely and the net caved in. Kemp thought he'd scored. Millington was too dazed to know.

That broken goalpost caused the first leg of the Chester–Plymouth first-round League Cup tie to be abandoned after 78 minutes. It became one of the few two-legged Cup ties to need a replay after the first leg. The score at the time was 2–2, Kemp having started the scoring, Steve Ludlam managing two for Chester and John Sims squaring the scores just a few minutes before the goal collapsed.

The teams met again at Chester the following week. The replay had one goal each in the first half, and they each had a goal to defend through the whole game … rather than just for 78 minutes. Another 1,700 spectators turned out (or was it the same 1,700 as the previous week?) but Chester had to fork out for a new goal and Plymouth bore the costs of another round-trip journey of over 500 miles (805km).

A broken goal doesn't necessarily mean the end of a game. It depends how easily the damage can be repaired. There was a seven-minute delay at Wolverhampton in January 1957 and a 45-minute delay at Lincoln in August 1970. I'm not sure what that says about modern technology. At

Lincoln they must have been tempted to muddle through as there were only a couple of minutes to play. Okay, lads, who's going to take off his shirt?

The 1957 incident at Wolverhampton is interesting for another reason. The opponents were Third Division Bournemouth, whose outside-left, Reg Cutler, ran into the netting, broke a goalpost, felt the net come down on top of him and lay tangled up like a caught fish. Cutler later scored the only goal of that fourth–round FA Cup tie to provide one of the shocks of the 1950s.

It takes two goals to make a game, and broken goalposts can strike the biggest of clubs. In 1971, Borussia Moechengladbach, leading the West German Bundesliga, were playing at home to Werder Bremen. The score was 1–1 when the game was abandoned two minutes from time after a goal apparatus had collapsed. Borussia lost the game by default, as they were held responsible for not having a replacement goal, but they won the league anyway.

SETTLED OUT OF COURT
DUNFERMLINE, OCTOBER 1981

St Johnstone won 2–1 at Dunfermline in a Scottish League First Division game but there was a matter left outstanding. It was resolved over two years later.

Jim Brown, Dunfermline's captain, had played the ball away when he was struck by John Pelosi's late leaping tackle. Pelosi's feet struck Brown at the front of the knee joint. Ligaments, tendons and muscles were severed below the knee. Despite two operations, it was the end of Brown's career, and he was forced to give up badminton and squash. Two years later the knee still gave him pain.

Pelosi, sent off for the tackle, was fined five weeks' wages and suspended for five weeks by St Johnstone. While away from the club he received a six-month suspension from the Scottish Football Association. Already that season Pelosi had been suspended for five matches after another sending-off incident.

Dunfermline Athletic could not raise a civil action on Jim Brown's behalf. Only he could do it, so Brown sued Pelosi as an individual and St Johnstone as an employer. Two sides of solicitors produced two interpretations of what was meant by 'reasonable care'. Brown claimed care should be in accordance with the accepted rules and conventions of football, that a player should keep control of his feet so as not to endanger other players and, above all, avoid striking a player on the leg with both feet at the same time.

Pelosi and St Johnstone claimed that the tackle could not be stopped. Also, they claimed that Brown, as a player, had freely and voluntarily agreed to accept the risk of injury in the normal course of the game.

The case did not reach court. St Johnstone made a settlement, believed to be around £20,000, and the rest of Scotland's professional clubs had a close look at their insurance policies.

TEAM ON STRIKE

MAIDSTONE, JANUARY 1983

On New Year's Day, Weymouth were scheduled to play an Alliance Premier League game at Maidstone. Weymouth players were on a high, having won their last nine games, but the club was on a low, pondering an overdraft of £50,000 and losing £700 a week.

Ten players in the squad were based around Bournemouth, 35 miles (56.3km) from Weymouth. These players travelled to games and training by car. They were costing the club over £200 in expenses, and the club had another idea.

Weymouth directors calculated that hiring a mini-bus for Bournemouth-based players would help save £100 a week, but the players thought such a mid-season change would be in breach of their contracts. They sought advice from the Professional Footballers' Association and decided to strike.

On the morning of the Maidstone game the Weymouth team coach set off at 8.30a.m. The driver was expecting to pick up the bulk of the squad at Ferndown, a few miles north of Bournemouth, a convenient meeting-place close to the main route east. Weymouth manager Stuart Morgan, Alliance Premier League manager of the month for December, was there. His Bournemouth-based players weren't. The coach had to turn round, and the game was postponed.

The strike lasted 48 hours. For a time it threatened the Monday home game with Bath City, Weymouth's tenth successive victory, and their third round FA Cup tie at Cambridge United, which resulted in a narrow 1–0 defeat.

The club reached a settlement by shelving the minibus idea and agreeing to go to arbitration. The Football Association mediated with an increase of £15 in Bournemouth-based players' weekly wages, in lieu of travel expenses. Almost all the players accepted this. The club had to face the consequences of failing to fulfil a fixture.

The Alliance Premier League fined Weymouth £100, ordered them to pay £895 to Maidstone for match expenses and losses and a further £182 towards the costs of the hearing. More controversially, Weymouth were docked ten league points, taking them out of the Championship race.

By March, when Weymouth's appeal was heard by the Football Association, the Dorset club's season was heading downhill. They had won only one of their last six games, they had to face the possible loss of ten league points and, at one away game, thieves had broken into their dressing-room during the game. A two-hour hearing at Lancaster Gate cleared the club of a charge of bringing the game into disrepute, ordered the fines and costs to stand, but, justifiably, agreed that the club should lose no league points. The FA offered the chance for three extra points, saying the match with Maidstone should be rearranged.

Maidstone won the game 3–0 but missed the Alliance Premier League Championship by a point. Weymouth ended their crazy season in seventh position.

THE MISSING 78 SECONDS

DERBY, MAY 1983

It was a troubled season for Derby County – only two wins in their first 22 League games and some major spots of bother, particularly in January, when games with Leeds United and Chelsea triggered serious crowd disturbances on successive Saturdays. By the last Saturday of the season, however, the club had rallied. A run of 15 unbeaten League games had pulled them on to the fringe of the relegation zone in Division Two. A win in the last game of the season, at home to Fulham, would ensure safety.

Fulham had their own interests. Malcolm Macdonald's young team had been in the top three for most of the season. A recent bad run had created anxiety, but a win at Derby would guarantee promotion to Division One at Leicester City's expense.

After 75 minutes' play Derby County's Bobby Davison volleyed the first goal of the game. A small pitch invasion by celebrating fans was soon cleared, but the crowd gathered around the edge of pitch, about five or six deep. The pitch became smaller.

Robert Wilson, a Fulham midfield player, was kicked by a spectator while the ball was in play. The touchlines were no longer visible. The referee, Ray Chadwick from Darwen, did his best under the circumstances. Then, when he blew his whistle for offside, the fans, thinking the game was over, swarmed on to the pitch to celebrate Derby's 1–0 win.

Referee Chadwick's watch showed 78 seconds still to play, but the teams had to leave the field. A second Fulham player, Jeff Hopkins, was assaulted in the process. He was too shocked to continue. The referee did not take the players back on to the pitch.

Fulham manager Malcolm Macdonald felt his team deserved a replay. He argued that it wasn't Fulham's fault that the crowd had invaded, cut the game by 78 seconds and interfered with some of the later minutes. Others felt that Derby had deserved to win, looked well on top and the chances of Fulham scoring two goals in the last 78 seconds were minimal. One national newspaper asked readers to recall all those games where away teams had scored two in the last 78 seconds after being one down.

The Football League ruled that the result should stand. Fulham appealed to the Football Association, but with no joy. The only tangible outcome was that Derby County were forced to spend money to improve the security of their ground. They erected perimeter fencing, which stayed a permanent fixture for almost six years.

STRANGE SUBSTITUTION
CAMBRIDGE, FEBRUARY 1984

There have been plenty of strange incidents involving substitutes. Sometimes a newcomer can immediately change the course of a game with a goal. Brendan O'Callaghan of Stoke City scored within ten seconds of coming on as a substitute for his debut (in 1979) and Joe Craig scored with his first touch in a Scottish international shirt (in 1977). On the debit side, at least two players, John Ritchie of Stoke (in 1972) and Bobby Houston of Kilmarnock (in 1979), have been sent off without touching the ball after coming on as substitutes, while John McAlle of Wolves broke a leg almost immediately after taking the field in a 1980 game.

The idea of substituting players during a game met ardent opposition in Britain before the authorities agreed in 1965 (in England) and 1966 (in Scotland). Once the notion of substituting solely for injured players was deemed unworkable, managers were left to contemplate all sorts of tactical options. My favourite is the one used by Cambridge City manager Bill Leivers during a game against Ashford in February 1984.

Leivers, a former Chesterfield and Manchester City full-back, had achieved success as Cambridge United manager, taking them from the Southern League to Division Three, before moving to Cambridge's other club via Chelmsford. He had also had spells as Doncaster Rovers' player-manager and Workington Town manager, and was not afraid to experiment. On 4 February, Cambridge City were 4–0 down to Ashford after 25 minutes' play. It was the second successive home game in which City had conceded four in the first half-hour, and, as they had lost the previous one 4–1, Leivers thought it was time to try something different … very different. He substituted goalkeeper, Nigel Ashman, switched midfield player Trevor Williams into goal, pushed central defender Geoff Hancocks up to centre-forward and dropped Phil Ashworth back from the forward-line to midfield. That left room for the substitute, a natural central defender.

Leivers felt he had to try something drastic to stop Ashford scoring 20 goals, although 19-year-old Ashman wasn't totally to blame for the poor start to the game.

The second half certainly brought the drastic change Leivers was looking for. Ashworth pulled one back, Hancocks got another, Gary French scored a third. That meant seven goals in the net at one end, none in the other. Cambridge City came back from 4–0 down but lost 4–3.

THE 68-HOUR GAME
FLORIDA, AUGUST–SEPTEMBER 1984

When Ernie Schultz, a Miami student, left the field with exhaustion at 9.20 pm on 2 September 1984 it was hardly surprising. At that point the game between North Palm Beach Golden Bears and Palm Beach Piranhas had been going for 51½ hours.

The game eventually lasted 68 hours and 11 minutes, thus breaking the record for the longest-ever game. During this time one player broke an arm and there were several cases of exhaustion, Schultz being the first. The game was finally stopped when one team was down to only six fit players. The teams were following international rules whereby they couldn't continue with fewer than six on one side.

The game, which started on 31 August, was a systematic attempt at a world record for long play. The previous record (65 hours 1 minute) had been set by the Callinafercy club in Ireland four years previously. In the Florida game, the players averaged 19 years of age. They took five-minute breaks every hour and changed uniform 22 times.

There was a problem at the start. Someone forgot to tell the local police, and when local residents complained of the noise the game was ordered to another field 6 miles (9.7km) away.

'WE WANT 20'

STIRLING, DECEMBER 1984

Stirling Albion had some trepidation about their first–round Scottish Cup tie at home to Selkirk. The previous season Stirling were sitting on a huge lead at the top of the Scottish Second Division when they lost 2–1 at home to Inverness Caledonian of the Highland League, the winning goal coming in the last minute of extra-time. Stirling's season had gone downhill from there. They missed the chance of a Cup tie at home to Rangers, and they missed out on promotion. Stirling were still in the Second Division when they were drawn against Selkirk of the Border Amateur League W Division. The prevailing opinion, supported by Stirling manager Alex Smith, was that the game shouldn't be taken lightly. It wouldn't be easy.

Stirling sent chief scout George Rankin to watch Selkirk. He saw them take a 3–0 lead at Leithen Rovers and left before the finish. He didn't see them concede five in the last 20 minutes and go down to a 5–3 defeat.

Stirling Albion, meanwhile, were scoring four in the last 15 minutes of their match at Albion Rovers. Both sides, unwittingly, were warming up for their next week's Cup match, which would establish a British record for the twentieth century. From the start to the end of the game, Stirling Albion showed no signs of undcrestimating their amateur opponents. Their five first-half goals were all scored by different players – Irvine (6 minutes), Maxwell

(12), Ormond (26), Thompson (34) and Dawson (36) – and Walker became the sixth Stirling player on the score-sheet shortly after half-time. Thereafter it was one long procession towards the Selkirk goal.

On another day, Selkirk goalkeeper Richard 'Midge' Taylor might have saved the thirteenth goal, and there was a suspicion of offside about the nineteenth, scored by Neil Watt. Otherwise, Stirling were pretty good value for their 20–0 win, and Taylor made some good saves to restrict the score to a score.

Stirling's second-half goalscoring was dominated by David Thompson, a £10,000 signing from Stenhousemuir, who scored six in the second half. The 20 goals were shared by eight players – David Thompson (7), Willie Irvine (5), Keith Walker (2), substitute Neil Watt (2), Scott Maxwell (1), Jimmy Ormond (1), Rab Dawson (1) and Gerry McTeague (1).

Selkirk player-manager Jackson Cockburn had the idea that his team might just be able to frustrate Stirling and catch them in the second half. There's no telling what would have happened had one of Selkirk's two shots gone in, or their one corner-kick had come to something. Towards the end, though, the dreams had been obliterated. I am reminded of a line in a report of Arbroath's 36–0 win over Bon Accord in 1885: 'After the twentieth goal, Bon Accord played like a team with no hope.'

There was a touching moment near the end, when Stirling's score was in the high teens. Selkirk officials on the touch-lines collected as many numbers as they could and held them up to indicate they wanted to substitute them all. It was a pity there weren't more than a few hundred spectators present to laugh at the joke. Stirling supporters, having chanted 'We want ten' after an hour's play, were able to chant 'We want 20' in the last few minutes. At the end manager Smith thought his team had scored 19 rather than 20 goals. It was an excusable mistake. It was very easy to miss a goal.

This was Stirling Albion's second record of the 1980s. The other was not so positive. They failed to score a goal in the last 13 Scottish League games of 1980–1, altogether playing 1,293 minutes between McPhee's goal (31 January 1981) and Torrance's goal on the opening day of the next season (29 August 1981). That was probably the point at which they started saving them up for poor Selkirk.

Stirling Albion could justifiably be proud of their achievement of recording the biggest victory in British soccer this century, but Selkirk, completely outclassed on the day, could also be proud. Theirs had been an incredible achievement to reach the first round of the Scottish Cup for the first time.

A POOCH OF A GOAL
STOKE-ON-TRENT, NOVEMBER 1985

To say a dog scored a goal is understating the case. It's almost like saying England scored a fourth in the 1966 World Cup Final when a forward tapped in a pass from a defender. So let's give the dog full credit. This was no everyday goal by a dog. This was supreme opportunism at its best.

David Hall, secretary of Knave of Clubs, recalls the most amazing thing he has ever seen on a football field: 'We were playing Newcastle Town in the Staffordshire Sunday Cup, and 1 think we were losing 2–0 at the time. One of our players was running down the field with only the goalkeeper to beat. He tried a shot from 15 yards (13.7m) out and miscued it, so it was going well wide. The dog ran on to the field, jumped up at the ball and headed it. The ball flew into the net.'

The dog, a mongrel, disappeared before either secretary had a chance to sign him. He left behind an argument which will continue for years. Should the referee give a goal? David Hall explains: 'There was quite a crowd at Monks Neil Park. Most were laughing at it, but a lot didn't know what the rules would say. The Newcastle players argued that the referee couldn't allow a goal, but the referee did. Our side rejoiced, but their players weren't too happy.'

Newcastle Town hung on to win the Cup tie 3–2.

Like star midfield players, dogs can arrive from nowhere and make an impact on games. They are usually good at keeping their eyes on the ball and dribbling it, but not many are as good in the air as the mongrel at Monks Neil Park. Unfortunately, for at least one footballer, dogs can also be strong tacklers. Chic Brodie was keeping goal for Brentford against Colchester in 1970 when a ferocious white mutt ran full pelt into him just as he was collecting a back-pass. The dog hit Brodie's left knee as he twisted and the goalkeeper suffered serious knee-ligament damage, enough to finish his career at Football League level. The nearest the goalkeepers' union came to exacting retribution on wildlife, as far as I'm aware, was a game in Holland. A high kick from the Feyenoord goalkeeper hit a pigeon which fell dead on to the field.

FIVE PENALTIES
IN A GAME
LONDON, MARCH 1989

Referee Kelvin Morton, an accountant from Bury St Edmunds, helped create a new British record when he awarded five penalties in a Division Two game between Crystal Palace and Brighton and Hove Albion. All five came in a 27-minute period either side of half-time.

It was an extraordinary game. Palace's first goal, in the twenty-third minute, was sparkling, Ian Wright hitting a volley some considerable distance from goal. When Brighton were reduced to ten men five minutes later – Mike Trusson was sent off for a foul on Eddie McGoldrick – Palace took complete control and earned three penalties in the space of five minutes just before half-time.

Mark Bright had taken over from Neil Redfearn as the Palace penalty-taker, and, in the last home match, he had scored with his first attempt. Bright's method used more power than subtlety. Against Brighton goalkeeper John Keeley he slammed in the first penalty to make the score 2–0, mishit the second penalty against Keeley's legs and opted not to take the third. Ian Wright obliged instead, and hit the ball against a post.

Six minutes after half-time Brighton themselves were granted a penalty – Alan Curbishley scored. Then Palace were awarded their fourth of the game. There was no shortage of willing takers. John Pemberton had a try. His shot went over the crossbar.

Brighton were considerably heartened by all this. Palace, on the other hand, having missed three penalties, still only 2–1 ahead, playing against ten men, worrying about their attempts to reach a Second Division play-off position, were growing agitated and nervous. A few more penalty misses might have inspired Brighton defenders to appeal for them in their own area while Palace players shouted 'Never, ref'. Brighton took advantage of Palace's loss of composure to make some late attacks, but Perry Suckling produced a couple of excellent saves and Crystal Palace hung on to win 2–1 when they should have won far more convincingly.

Prior to this Palace–Brighton game, there had been at least five games with four penalty-kicks – St Mirren–Rangers (1904), Burnley–Grimsby (1909), Crewe–Bradford (1924), Northampton–Hartlepool (1976) and Bristol City–Wolves (1977). In addition, other games with a concentration of penalties have certainly occurred outside Britain, including the Argentina–Mexico World Cup game in 1930 when five penalties (some disputed) were awarded. The Palace–Brighton game, on the other hand, aroused no real complaints about the referee's decisions. Palace manager Steve Coppell had only one misgiving – he felt his team should have scored with all four kicks rather than one. As a warning to them not to lose their composure again, he invited them back for extra training the day after the game.

A FLARE-UP FOR FIFA
RIO DE JANEIRO, SEPTEMBER 1989

The FIFA general secretary called it 'the biggest attempt at swindle in the history of FIFA'. It happened midway through the second half of a World Cup qualifying game between Brazil and Chile. Brazil led 1–0 at the time, and looked certain to qualify for the 1990 World Cup Finals. A draw was all Brazil needed, whereas Chile had to win.

Brazil had dominated the game to that point. Careca's goal, on the hour, was small reward for all the Brazilian pressure, but good goalkeeping by Roberto Rojas, the Chilean captain, had kept the lead to one. Rojas was also the principal actor in the drama which followed an incident in the sixty-ninth minute.

A 24-year-old Brazilian woman spectator threw a green signal-flare into the Chilean goalmouth while play was at the other end. It floated down, and a cloud of smoke appeared near the goalkeeper Rojas, who fell to the ground holding his face. Chilean players and medical officials gathered round the fallen goalkeeper, and, rather than wait for an official stretcher, they clumsily carried Rojas off the field. The goalkeeper appeared to be bleeding heavily from a cut on the face.

The rest of the Chilean team followed Rojas to the dressing-room. The Brazilian players stood around talking, and match officials waited. When spectators showed signs of impatience, troops were sent to the dressing-room to investigate. FIFA delegates soon joined them. Chile had decided to withdraw from the match, considering lives to be in danger, and the match therefore had to be abandoned. Thousands of the 160,000 spectators waited, many for as long as two hours, in hope that the game would be resumed.

The Chilean team doctor reported that Rojas had required five stitches in a facial cut, but the Brazilians claimed that the blood was simulated. Experts argued that signal-flares were harmless, whereas fireworks might cause such an injury. Photographs showed the flare had not hit Rojas and no blood was initially visible. A FIFA investigation confirmed the deception. Rojas admitted that he had faked his signal-flare injury.

FIFA suspended Rojas from national and international football for life. They also suspended several Chilean officials, including the team doctor, who had issued a false medical certificate, and the equipment official, who had disposed of the goalkeeper's gloves and jersey. Chile were banned from the 1994 World Cup Finals, while Brazilian authorities received a small fine for failing to make adequate security arrangements. Brazil were awarded a 2–0 forfeit victory.

History has shown that a team failing to complete a fixture is likely to be in serious trouble with the football authorities. Later that same month, September 1989, while the Brazil–Chile decision was still being settled, an English non-League team walked off the field. Dunstable Town player-manager Kevin Millett was incensed at a referee who sent off three of his team-mates during an FA Cup tie against Staines Town. He led off the remaining seven, and the tie was abandoned after 38 minutes.

FOOTBALL FOR PIGS

VARIOUS PIG FARMS IN BRITAIN, FROM JUNE 1990

While the world's football press concentrated on seemingly strange events, like Cameroon's defeat of World Cup holders Argentina, something was stirring at the grassroots of football. More and more pigs were taking up the game.

When Bernard Hoggarth visited the Paris Agricultural Show early in the year, he spotted a Danish product, the Domino Stress Ball, which enabled pigs to play football. Hoggarth bought some balls for his pig business at Cranswick Mill, near Driffield in Yorkshire, and, after successful trials, began marketing Stress Balls in Britain. The manufacturers claim that football-playing pigs are less aggressive and less stressed and therefore happier and more likely to put on weight. You may have heard the same argument applied to human footballers.

The product was publicised around the time of the 1990 World Cup Finals. There were suggestions that an international team of pigs should be managed by Franz Baconbauer, and an English Premier Cut League should include Trotterham Hotspur, Queen's Pork Rangers and Roast Ham United. It would appeal to those football-club groundsmen who claim they've seen dressing-rooms looking like pig-sties.

Pigs are intelligent creatures. When bored, they can become aggressive, and bite the tails or ears of other pigs in the pen. Hence the need to amuse them. Traditionally, some pig-keepers have suspended chains or left cans in pens to chew on. The Stress Ball is a more sophisticated toy. 'They roll it around the sty, shoot it into corners and leap over it on their way to their fodder,' says the promotion literature. In practice, pigs rely more on dribbling with their snouts than kicking the ball.

Stress Balls are indestructible. They are bright red, about eight or nine inches in diameter and made of sturdy plastic. Each one has a ball-bearing in the middle which rattles as the pigs knock the ball around the pen. A Stress Ball needs to be disinfected and cleaned after each batch of pigs, but can be used time and time again.

On his Yorkshire pig farm, Bernard Hoggarth experimented with one ball in a pen of about 15 pigs. The pigs tended to play with the ball on their own and when one had had enough another took over. No doubt this ability to pass the ball at the right moment can be developed further. Perhaps we will eventually see pigs playing team games, and spectators guaranteed lots of excitement around the pen areas.

It sounds like something out of *Animal Farm*, doesn't it? Those familiar with George Orwell's satirical fairy tale may recall that the pigs learned to read, lead and stand on hind legs, and *Animal Farm* became a replica of the human society it had replaced. A manager of a soccer team of pigs would be especially vulnerable to the chop.

Stress Balls have also been supplied to breeding stables for racehorses to play with, but a well-hoofed shot could cause damage if it hit a passing spectator. At the time of going to press chickens had yet to be approached: the manufacturers were worried about too many fouls.

A RE-ENACTMENT GAME

BRADFORD, SEPTEMBER 1991
AND THEN ANNUALLY ON CUP FINAL DAY

On the night that Bradford City beat Newcastle United 3–2, supporters of the two clubs gathered in the Fountain Inn on Bradford's Heaton Road. The pub was the headquarters of the Heaton branch of the Bradford City Supporters Club and also of the Yorkshire branch of the Newcastle United Supporters Club.

'And we beat you in the 1911 Cup Final,' said one Bradford City fan.

'But that Cup Final goal was offside,' said a Newcastle fan.

Suddenly the conversation was more about the 1911 FA Cup Final than how that evening's result might affect City's chances of relegation or Newcastle's promotion aspirations. The Bradford City fans were aware of two recent events: a replica 1911 Cup Final shirt had been offered for sale; and the supporters club had been contacted by Richard Edwards of Coventry, who claimed to be a relative of Jimmy Speirs, scorer of the 1911 goal which gave Bradford City a 1–0 victory over Newcastle United.

Wouldn't it be a good idea to replay the 1911 FA Cup Final with a game between rival supporters?

The two sets of fans worked hard at arranging a re-enactment game, supported by the two clubs and the local newspaper. Bradford City offered the use of Valley Parade, but the date had to be changed from Tuesday 17 September to Sunday 29 September when a Rumbelows

Cup game interfered. The Beamish Museum in County Durham helped to organise Newcastle United's replica kit, and special replica shirts were made for the Bradford lads. The 1911 ball was brought out of its showcase for publicity pictures and a replica programme was printed. On the day of the match, players sported period slicked-back hairstyles and false moustaches. The Newcastle United goalkeeper wore an authentic flat cap and City manager Philip Metcalfe dressed in bowler-hat and long coat.

The major beneficiary was the Burns Research Unit at Bradford University. It was just over six years since a tragic fire at Valley Parade had killed 55 people and injured 210 others. The programme sales for the re-enactment 1911 Cup Final raised £800.

Bradford City fan Mark Neale, the match organiser, later described the build-up in a special issue of the *City Gent* fanzine: 'In the dressing room, as the teams got changed, we found ourselves the subject of much media attention as we dressed in the replica kits. Out on the pitch I was photographed from every angle holding the 1911 ball, and we really did not have time to savour the moment. As I went back into the dressing room, the teams were coming out at the request of the press for yet another photo. As a result we ended up on the pitch without any balls for the warm-up, without the match officials, and with me bursting to go to the loo! The rest, as they say, is history, although you could say that it's "recycled history" in this case.'

Neale and his team-mates were fulfilling a lifelong ambition of playing for City in a Cup Final at Valley Parade, although Neale would have preferred the game not to have started while he was still bursting for a pee. City mascot James Hodgkinson kicked off with the genuine 1911 ball. His great-grandfather Jimmy McDonald, Bradford City captain in 1911, would have kicked the same ball, which was quickly replaced by a modern equivalent.

Newcastle had the better of the first half and led 1–0 at

the interval. The Bradford boys equalised in the second half. The game looked to be petering towards a 1–1 draw when the referee controversially awarded a late penalty to Newcastle. The penalty was converted and Newcastle won 2–1.

'It was never a penalty,' said the City lads after the game. 'We'll have to play it again.'

And so they have. The game is now played annually on Manningham Mills on the morning of FA Cup Final Day. The two sets of supporters continue to be friendly, and the bond was strengthened when professionals like John Hendrie and Peter Jackson played for both clubs. After each game, the two teams retire to the Fountain Inn to watch the Cup Final. The only exceptions, of course, come when Newcastle United reach the real FA Cup Final and the re-enactment match is delayed by a week.

Think of the fun the next time Bradford City and Newcastle United meet in the FA Cup Final.

PICKING THE
WRONG PLAYERS
STUTTGART, LEEDS AND BARCELONA,
SEPTEMBER AND OCTOBER 1992

'The manager picked the wrong players,' supporters moan
when their team is knocked out of a Cup competition.
Sometimes they are right. The most obvious example was
the first round of the 1992–3 European Cup competition
when VfB Stuttgart coach Uwe Hoeness indisputably
picked the wrong players for the second leg of the tie against
Leeds United.

Stuttgart won the home leg 3–0 and looked to be coasting in
the return when Buck's thirty-third minute goal equalised
an earlier effort by Gary Speed. Leeds continued to attack,
however, and a Gary McAllister penalty just before half-time,
a lob from Eric Cantona (60 minutes) and a Lee Chapman
header from Gordon Strachan's corner (79 minutes) made
the score 4–1 on the night. It set up an exciting last ten
minutes but there were no further goals. The second leg
ended with the scores level (4–4) and Stuttgart winners on
the away goal.

Meanwhile, in Germany, alert television viewers had
quickly spotted that it was Hoeness rather than Leeds
manager Howard Wilkinson who had chosen the wrong
players to do the job. The appearance of Adrian Knup and
Jovo Simanic, two late substitutes, confirmed that the squad
contained four foreign players when the maximum was
three. The German television station showing the game
was inundated with calls pointing out the mistake. The

rule was broken when Hoeness named his squad: 'The 16 or fewer players chosen by a club to take part in any match under competition rules ... should not include more than three players who are not eligible to play for the national association with which the club is registered.'

Clubs were given clear guidance as to what constituted a foreign player and what was an 'assimilated player'. The latter included players raised through a youth policy and players with five years at the club. Leeds United had three foreign players – Eric Cantona (France), Gary McAllister (Scotland) and Gordon Strachan (Scotland) – but Welshman Gary Speed was not considered foreign because he had been through the Leeds United training system.

The Stuttgart case was quite different. They quite clearly had four foreign players in the squad – Slobodan Dubajic (Serbia), Eyjolfur Sverrisson (Iceland), Adrian Knup (Switzerland) and Jovo Simanic (Serbia) – and the club admitted the mistake the day after the second leg at Elland Road. This was a very different case from the one that had occurred in Holland in the 1990–1 season. Feyenoord had then made a substitution which gave them three foreigners on the field during the game with Tilburg when the maximum permitted was two. The substitute was sent off and Feyenoord continued with ten men.

The Leeds–Stuttgart revelation caused a tricky problem for UEFA, who pondered over it for several days. Two options were available: disqualify Stuttgart from the competition and award the tie to Leeds United; or follow precedents and award Leeds a 3–0 home win. The four-man UEFA committee were split down the middle. After five hours of deliberation the two in favour of disqualification agreed to award a 3–0 win.

With the 3–0 home success the scores were level at 3–3 but Leeds United were still owed the chance of playing extra-time on their own ground. A 30-minute session at Elland Road would have constituted a really strange game, but instead the tie went to a replay on neutral ground. After mention of various locations – Basle, Berne and Rotterdam – the third leg of the tie was played at the Bernebeu Stadium, Barcelona.

On Friday 9 October a crowd of 10,000 rattled around the 120,000 stadium and watched as a late goal from substitute Carl Shutt brought Leeds a 2–1 victory. Shortly afterwards, though, Leeds were knocked out for a second time, beaten 4–2 on aggregate by Glasgow Rangers of Scotland in the second round.

'ONE TEAM IN TALLINN'
TALLINN, ESTONIA, OCTOBER 1996

Having beaten Latvia 2–0 in Riga on 5 October, the Scotland party flew to Tallinn in readiness for their next Group 4 World Cup qualifying match – against Estonia on 9 October.

The two countries had a good football relationship: Scottish fans had enjoyed visiting Estonia when the teams met in a 1993 World Cup qualifier and some of them had even returned to see the Estonia–Croatia game; Estonian officials had visited the Scottish Football Association to improve their understanding of football administration; and the SFA had sent equipment for Estonian youngsters. Yes, the two nations had a good rapport ... until Scottish officials saw the floodlights in the Kadriorg Stadium.

In preparation for the 6.45p.m. kick-off, Estonian officials had arranged for temporary floodlighting to be brought from Finland. Scotland complained to FIFA that the low-level floodlights, mounted on lorries, would cause problems for goalkeepers when dealing with crosses from one particular side. It was reminiscent of floodlight debates in the 1950s.

The next morning, at nine o'clock, FIFA announced that the time of the game would be changed from 6.45p.m. to 3p.m. Scottish officials ran round all the local haunts to spread news to their fans, buses were hired to ferry supporters to the ground and the players' preparations were changed accordingly. However, the Estonian officials pleaded that they had far more to consider – security arrangements in the stadium, consideration of supporters who were working during the day and the location of the players (50 miles/80km from the ground). The most important thing, however, was the television contract, which had been arranged for a 6.45p.m. kick-off.

Scotland manager Craig Brown fully expected Estonia to conform with FIFA's ruling, so he went ahead with the preparations. Just before three o'clock John Collins led out Scotland but the opposition had still not arrived.

'One team in Tallinn,' sang the Scotland supporters. 'There's only one team in Tallinn.'

The Scotland players lined up for the kick-off. The referee, Miroslav Radoman of Yugoslavia, is probably the only referee in history who had to be certain that players couldn't be offside from a kick-off. (They must be inside their own half or the place-kick is retaken.) He blew the whistle and Billy Dodds tapped the ball to Collins.

The referee blew his whistle again. The match was over.

Tosh McKinlay punched the air and raised his hands to the Scottish fans. Scotland thought they must have won the game by default as a FIFA directive stated that teams would win 3–0 if the opposition failed to turn up.

'Easy, easy, easy,' chanted the supporters.

No caps were awarded but the Scottish players were allowed to keep their shirts. They couldn't very well swap them with the opposition, could they?

As for the two teams:

Estonia:
Scotland: Goram, McNamara, Boyd, Calderwood, McKinlay, Burley, Lambert, Collins, McGinlay, Dodds, Jackson.

The Estonia team bus arrived at the Kadriorg Stadium at five o'clock. They were too late for the game, such as it was.

On 7 November the World Cup organising committee met and decided that the Estonia–Scotland tie should be replayed on neutral ground. There was some disquiet about this decision, not least because the chair of the committee, Lennart Johansson, came from Sweden, and Sweden were in the same group as Scotland and Estonia. Scotland felt they (and their fans) were being punished for something that was no fault of their own. On 27 November it was announced that the re-match would take place in Monaco.

The next month the English Premier League had to deal with a similar situation when Middlesbrough failed to turn up for a match at Blackburn Rovers, claiming that 23 players were ill or injured. Middlesbrough were later deducted three points and fined £50,000, even though no formal directive seemed to exist. When that game was re-arranged, the two teams drew 0–0. The two lost points caused Middlesbrough to be relegated.

Estonia finally played Scotland on 4 February 1997. Scottish fans turned up with miners, glasses and special spectacles with torches to mock the floodlight farce in Tallinn. Scotland's only good spell came late in the first half. Duncan Ferguson's header was scrambled off the line, Tom Boyd's shot hit the crossbar, and Estonia goalkeeper Mart Poom made two wonderful saves. The match ended 0–0 but Scotland went on to qualify for France '98 as the best second-place finishers in the European groups.

AS YOU WERE, LADS

CLEVEDON, SOMERSET, OCTOBER 1996

Witney Town and Clevedon Town were drawn together in a two-legged Dr Martens Cup first-round tie. The first leg was at Witney.

Adams scored for Witney in the twenty-fifth minute but a Jackson penalty levelled the scores. Witney had the better of the game but failed to get a winner. Indeed, only a last-minute save from Witney goalkeeper Alder saved the home side from defeat. The match ended 1–1.

'Clevedon's away goal could be crucial,' wrote Jon Adaway in the *Oxford Mail*. 'Witney must score in the second leg or face a quick exit.'

Later that same month Witney travelled to Clevedon for the second leg. The teams were again well-matched.

Adams scored for Witney in the seventieth minute, but Winstone equalised eight minutes later. The second leg also finished 1–1. Extra-time followed.

In the one hundred and twelfth minute Winstone gave Clevedon the lead directly from a corner-kick but Crouch immediately equalised for Witney. The match ended 2–2 after extra-time.

The scores were level at the end of extra-time but Witney now had two away goals. At 10.05p.m., the teams left the pitch and the spectators set off for home. Witney were through to the next round on away goals.

Or were they?

While the teams washed and dressed, the referee and the Clevedon Town secretary were speaking on the telephone to the secretary of the Dr Martens League. They all studied the rule-book and discussed the consequences. It appeared that away goals only counted double if they were scored in normal time. The correct ruling after 1–1 and 2–2 (after extra-time) was a penalty shoot-out.

Everybody back on the pitch.

Witney Town players were about to board their coach when officials went in with the bad news.

'You have to go back for a penalty shoot-out, lads.' You can imagine how footballers would react to this.

'Come off it, Boss.'

'Pull the other one.'

Or words with similar meaning.

Eventually they realised that it was true. The players changed back into their dirty kit and went back out. A handful of spectators gathered behind one goal. One Witney official later described the whole scene as something akin to village football.

At 10.30p.m. a rather embarrassed referee began the penalty shoot-out. No doubt he would have sympathised with his counterpart in the 1895 FA Cup tie between Barnsley St Peters and Liverpool. Liverpool won that match 2–1 after extra-time only to learn later that the referee should not have played extra-time. The score was changed back to 1–1 and the teams replayed at Liverpool. Fortunately, Liverpool won the replay 4–0.

Fortunately again, for continuity's sake, Witney won the shoot-out 4–2 with successful shots by Caffel, Rouse, Phillips and Adams. Witney were now definitely through to the next round although the players found it hard to celebrate twice. They were also a little suspicious.

'Maybe it will go to a replay after all.' But it didn't.

WATCHING A DIFFERENT GAME

CHELTENHAM, FEBRUARY 1998

Every year I try to visit Cheltenham in Gloucestershire, where my father learned his football. I retrace his steps by walking along Prestbury Road and turning off towards the Whaddon Road Recreation Ground. Here, in the late 1920s, my father first played organised football. Wearing the red, yellow and black hoops of Charlton Kings School, he played in Steve Bloomer boots and chased the ball wherever it went.

I always look at Whaddon Road Recreation Ground and think about watching a match there someday. Instead I usually saunter across the road, to the home of Cheltenham Town FC, where my father once played against teams like Birmingham Trams, Newport County Reserves and (in a one-off friendly) Tranmere Rovers. I pay my money and walk around the terraces, looking across at the hills where my father had once played his own form of strange soccer.

This was my routine on Saturday 14 February 1998, when I became part of a crowd of 2,580 people gathering to watch a GM Vauxhall Conference match between Cheltenham and Stevenage Borough. Stevenage were that season's FA Cup giant-killers, having beaten Cambridge United (second round) and Swindon (third round) before taking Premier League Newcastle United to a replay.

The two teams warmed up on the pitch and then went back inside. Just before three o'clock they came out and kicked around. Then there was an odd delay.

'Maybe the referee's not turned up,' someone said.

Eventually, several minutes after the appointed kick-off time, the referee came out and talked to both managers. The players left the pitch. It was announced that there would be a ten-minute delay before starting the game. The Stevenage players came out to warm up for the third time.

Then came the next announcement.

'Could you please evacuate the ground and congregate on the Whaddon Road Recreation Ground.'

A security alert.

We left the ground in an orderly fashion, fans of both clubs side by side, all wearing red-and-white. As we left the ground we realised that there was a game to watch. Two Northern Senior League teams, Crescent United and Hardwicke, were playing on the Whaddon Road Recreation Ground. Their match was about ten minutes old. Suddenly their crowd of half a dozen was swelled to well over a thousand. An innate love of football burst forth as supporters of Cheltenham and Stevenage surrounded the pitch and hammed up their presence with exaggerated sounds from the touch-lines.

'Ooooooooooohhh.' 'Aaaaaaaahhhhhhhhhh.'

The surprised local players ran around at twice the speed and fought for the ball like tigers. An innocuous trip brought a free-kick.

'Off, off, off, off, off,' chanted the crowd in unison.

Then the Cheltenham fans recognised one of their former players, Mark Buckland, who was playing for Crescent at the age of 36.

'There's only one Mark Buckland,' the fans sang in chorus, and Buckland must have been thinking back to the early 1980s, when he played for Wolves in the old First Division. When Crescent's Nick Davies headed an excellent goal, it was greeted with cheers and applause. A save from the Hardwicke goalkeeper was as good as anything you would see anywhere. More applause.

We watched the rest of the first half and then filed back across the road, where the Stevenage players were warming up for the fourth time.

The Vauxhall Conference match started an hour late and ended 1–1. Dale Watkins scored in the first half for Cheltenham and Dean Wordsworth equalised with a last-minute penalty. But the Northern Senior League game was more memorable for me. Maybe I should have stayed on the Whaddon Recreation Ground and watched Crescent United beat Hardwicke 2–1.

TENSION AT WEMBLEY

LONDON, MAY 1998

The stakes were high when Charlton Athletic and Sunderland met in the 1998 Division One play-off final. Promotion to the Premier League would guarantee an additional £7 million in television revenue plus extra attendance receipts and merchandising sales.

Sunderland had missed automatic promotion by one point, while Charlton had finished two points further behind in fourth place. Charlton arrived at Wembley having not conceded a goal in their last nine games, including two 1–0 victories against Ipswich in the play-off semi-final. Sunderland had beaten Sheffield United 3–2 on aggregate in their semi-final. Everyone was expecting a close game – Charlton and Sunderland had played two League draws that season – but no one forecast just how close.

Viewed from a long-term perspective, the idea of a play-off final was still fairly strange. And what would previous generations have made of all the trimmings? There were flame-throwers and ticker-tape welcomes for the teams as they left the tunnel. The players walked past ubiquitous advertising boards and a sea of red-and-white striped replica Sunderland shirts decorated the area behind the tunnel.

The sponsor's portable centre-circle carpet – it pays to decide NATIONWIDE – was peeled away and the two teams began their forty-ninth League match of the season.

The most significant feature of the first 18 minutes was three cautions.

Then Charlton's Clive Mendonca turned his marker and shot right-footed past the falling Lionel Perez. It was Mendonca's twenty-sixth goal of the season and put Charlton ahead at half-time. The irony was that Mendonca had supported Sunderland during his childhood. He had gone to the same school as Sunderland's Michael Gray and had played for Sunderland Schoolboys.

Sunderland turned the game their way with two goals in seven minutes early in the second half. Niall Quinn met Summerbee's corner with a powerful low header which went in at the near post and then Kevin Phillips scampered free to finish with a gentle flick over goalkeeper Ilic for his thirty-fifth of the season.

Clive Mendonca produced three superb touches when he equalised in the seventy-first minute. He guided a long ball from Keith Jones past the nearest defender, controlled it with the sole of his boot and then steered it past Perez. But Niall Quinn emulated Mendonca's two goals when he put Sunderland 3–2 ahead two minutes later, chesting down a long cross from the right and then scoring at the near post with his left foot. Substitute Daniele Dichio might have made it 4–2 shortly afterwards but miscued his shot from Summerbee's pass. Instead, after Perez had made a brilliant reflex save from Bright's deflection, Richard Rufus scored his first goal for Charlton (in 145 games) when he headed in a corner with only five minutes left.

The excitement continued in extra-time as tension rose among the 77,739 crowd. Or those who had stayed. One Charlton fan later confessed he had walked out at 3–2 because he couldn't take any more.

Quinn's lay-off allowed Summerbee to shoot Sunderland's fourth from the edge of the area (99 minutes) but Mendonca scored Charlton's third equaliser when he met a Steve Jones cross with his back to goal and turned sharply to score (103 minutes). Mendonca's hat-trick was the first in a play-off Final and Charlton fans would later debate which was the best goal of the three.

Tired legs played out the remainder of extra-time.

Charlton Athletic 4 Sunderland 4. And so to a penalty shoot-out.

Back to 0–0.

Mendonca scored for Charlton from the first penalty. Summerbee scored for Sunderland.

1–1.

Steve Brown scored for Charlton. Johnston for Sunderland.

2–2.

Keith Jones for Charlton. Kevin Ball for Sunderland. 3–3.

Kinsella scored for Charlton.

Makin scored for Sunderland … but only just as Ilic dived low to his right and palmed the ball into the net.

4–4.

Again.

Bowen for Charlton. Alex Rae for Sunderland. 5–5.

Sudden death. Robinson for Charlton. Quinn for Sunderland. 6–6.

Charlton goalkeeper Sasa Ilic had found a twopence coin on the pitch at the start of the shoot-out and was tossing it between kicks to keep busy. Now he threw it away. It wasn't working.

Shaun Newton scored for Charlton.

And then, after 13 right-footed penalties in the shoot-out, Sunderland's Michael Gray stepped forward with the first left-footed kick, low to Ilic's left. The goalkeeper dived and pushed it out. Seconds later he was buried under a pyramid of colleagues as Charlton Athletic celebrated promotion to the Premier League.

It was now 5.50p.m., three hours since the teams had first come out.

There were claims that this was Wembley's greatest game but a few other 4–4 draws are candidates. England shared eight goals with a team representing the Rest of Europe in 1953–4, and Guiseley and Gresley Rovers drew 4–4 in the 1991 FA Vase Final. I watched the latter and can vouch for its entertainment. Gresley and Guiseley were so closely matched that the amalgam 'Gruisly' appeared on the Wembley scoreboard during extra-time. Gresley came back from a 3–0 deficit to equalise in the last minute of normal time and then Guiseley equalised in the dying moments of extra-time. Guiseley won the replay 3–1.

The Charlton–Sunderland game is a strange game for two reasons other than a 4–4 draw at Wembley. The penalty shoot-out scoreline of 7–6 is what Anthony Fowles calls 'a scoreline of mystical significance to Charlton fans' in his book Welling to Wembley. Charlton, of course, had once beaten Huddersfield Town 7–6 in a 1957 League game (see page 98).

The second oddity is that so many millions could rest on one penalty-kick when the two teams were so obviously equal.

GOALKEEPER'S GOAL SAVES CARLISLE UNITED

CARLISLE, MAY 1999

'How long, Ref?' asked Carlisle United captain David Brightwell.

'Ten seconds,' the referee replied. 'This is your last chance.' Carlisle United had won a corner-kick in the fourth minute of stoppage-time. They were drawing their match against Plymouth Argyle 1–1 but needed to win to preserve their Nationwide League Division Three status. All 11 players went up for the corner, including goalkeeper Jimmy Glass.

It had been a desperate week for Carlisle fans. On the Wednesday Scarborough had beaten Plymouth 3–0 to take their tally to 47 points, one more than Carlisle. It was the first time all season that Carlisle had been bottom of the table and the circumstances were ominous for the final Saturday. As Carlisle had scored only 41 goals to Scarborough's 49, it meant they had to win their last game at home to Plymouth to have any hope of saving themselves. The bottom club would be relegated, their place taken by Cheltenham Town, already promoted from the Nationwide Conference.

Scarborough drew their last match – 1–1 against Peterborough – and their fans celebrated when they heard that Carlisle were drawing in stoppage-time.

It was a tense game at Brunton Park, Carlisle, played in front of a 7,500 crowd. Plymouth had lost Paul Gibb with a broken leg, and had taken the lead just after half-time through Lee Phillips. Then David Brightwell had equalised superbly from 25 yards (22.9m) in the sixty-second minute. And that seemed the end of the scoring ... until the fourth minute of stoppage-time.

Goalkeeper Jimmy Glass, 25, had been signed on loan from Swindon Town in time to play the last three games of the season. Carlisle had been given special permission by the League to sign him after transferring goalkeeper Tony Caig and suffering further injuries after the transfer deadline. Scarborough later unsuccessfully contested the signing.

When it was obvious that the late corner-kick was Carlisle's last chance, the crowd behind Glass's goal shouted for him to get up the field. When manager Nigel Pearson waved Glass forward, the goalkeeper made a late run. Nearly 100 yards (91m).

The corner came across. Carlisle's Scott Dobie jumped in front of a defender and powered a header towards goal. Plymouth goalkeeper James Dungey parried the ball. And there was goalkeeper Glass, 6 yards (5.5m) out, still running. He met the loose ball with a crisp right-foot shot and scored.

Skipper David Brightwell saw the red goalkeeping shirt amidst the blue and green of the two teams and didn't realise at first that Glass had come up for the corner. He thought it was a fan on the pitch.

Suddenly Glass was lying on the floor under a crowd of players.

'I think I've just scored the winner,' Glass said.

In the Main Stand a blind Carlisle fan called David Ross heard his friend's commentary of the match give way to an almighty roar. But it was only later that Ross could comprehend that the goal had been scored by the goalkeeper.

Glass jogged back towards his own penalty area but the referee blew the final whistle immediately. Fans rushed on and Glass was chaired off the pitch.

'Four minutes into injury time, he saved a team in a way that no goalkeeper has ever saved anything before,' wrote Anthony Ferguson in the *Carlisle News & Star*.

On the Monday after the game Jimmy Glass handed over his size-ten boots so that a bronze sculpture could be made of them for display in the city's planned Millennium Gallery. Carlisle fans bought T-shirts ('I believe in miracles') and other souvenirs of the incident. Meanwhile, Plymouth players could spend their summer thinking how best to mark goalkeepers from corner-kicks.

SENT-OFF PLAYER SUBSTITUTED

BIRKENHEAD, MERSEYSIDE, JANUARY 2000

First Division Tranmere Rovers were that season's Cup giant-killers. In the FA Cup fourth round, they led 1–0 against Premier League Sunderland, with two minutes of stoppage-time already played, when Clint Hill (Tranmere) fouled Alex Rae (Sunderland) in the Tranmere half. Hill was sent off by referee Rob Harris for a second cautionable offence. There was just enough time for Sunderland to launch a free-kick into the Tranmere penalty area.

In the dug-out area, the fourth official, David Unsworth, was dealing with the raging Hill, two managers (Peter Reid of Sunderland and John Aldridge of Tranmere Rovers) and two assistants (Adrian Heath and Kevin Sheedy). Before the Sunderland free-kick could be taken, Unsworth held up the board to signify a Tranmere substitution, but the board flashed the number six (Hill's number). Stephen Frail came on for Tranmere but nobody went off. Rovers still had 11 players on the field and Hill had been sent off.

Play resumed and the Sunderland free-kick was taken. A Sunderland player, under pressure from substitute Frail, headed the ball wide. Then the referee blew for full-time.

That left a quandary – should the match be replayed?

Starting with the Arsenal–Sheffield United replay, the authorities had had to make a number of difficult decisions about Cup ties. An FA Cup second qualifying round tie between Herne Bay and Farnham had been replayed after

Herne Bay used four substitutes instead of three in the original tie (September 1999). West Ham United had been told to replay a Worthington Cup quarter-final against Aston Villa for fielding an ineligible player (December 1999). One of the Hammers' substitutes, Manny Omoyinmi, who came on for the last eight minutes, had already played for Gillingham in the Worthington Cup earlier that season. West Ham lost the replay 3–1 after winning the first game (5–4 on penalties). Two staff members resigned over the Omoyinmi incident.

In the Tranmere–Sunderland case, the FA allowed the 1–0 result to stand. Sunderland manager Peter Reid had magnanimously credited Tranmere with winning the game 'fair and square'. Referee Rob Harris was suspended for two months.

Tranmere Rovers continued their FA Cup run by winning 2–1 at Fulham in the fifth round before losing 3–2 at home to Newcastle United in the sixth. That same season Rovers beat two Premiership teams – Coventry City and Middlesbrough – on the way to a Worthington Cup Final against Leicester City. Tranmere lost 2–1 to Leicester and Clint Hill was sent off again.

It was not long before Tranmere Rovers were involved in another strange match. In April 2003 they were leading Mansfield Town 2–0 only for the Division Two match to be abandoned at half-time. A fan had climbed on to the roof of a stand and refused to come down. Police decided to vacate the ground and, with the aid of the fire service, went on to the roof and helped the spectator down. The match was replayed two days later with Tranmere Rovers winning 3–1.

AUSTRALIA 31
AMERICAN SAMOA 0
COFF'S HARBOUR, AUSTRALIA, APRIL 2001

Having set a world record for a competitive international two days previously, by beating Tonga 22–0, the Australian national team went nine better against American Samoa in another Oceania World Cup qualifying group game.

American Samoa fielded a severely weakened team. Almost all of manager Tony Langkilde's original squad were ineligible because they did not have American passports, and most of his under-20 squad were unavailable as they were revising for exams. Langkilde ended up with a young team (average age 19) which included one 15 year old.

With a population of only 65,000, the American Samoa manager had a restricted choice anyway. In fact, FIFA rated American Samoa two hundred and third out of 203 countries.

At half-time the Australian Socceroos led 16–0 but were told to be professional in the second half. It was soon clear that American Samoa would suffer their record defeat, eclipsing the 18–0 loss in Tahiti the previous June, and their only hope would be for Australia to declare. American Samoa's only attack came in the eighty-sixth minute when Australia's goalkeeper Michael Petkovic saved a shot from Pati Feagiai. But Australia led 29–0 by then.

In a flurry of late scoring the scoreboard operator flashed up a 32–0 scoreline but the referee corrected him later. Archie Thompson scored 13 goals, a world record for an international player. The previous record holders had been Sofus Nielsen (Denmark in 1908) and Gottfried Fuchs (Germany in 1912) with ten in a match. Other than Australia, only Kuwait – against Bhutan in 2000 – have reached 20 goals in a match.

Australia went on to beat the winners of the other Oceanic Group (New Zealand) but lost 3–1 on aggregate to the fifth-placed South American team (Uruguay). Despite scoring 73 goals, Australia missed out on the 2004 World Cup Finals.

Teams like American Samoa have to start somewhere. Sark (population 550) is another small community that does well to field a team. In the 2003 Island Games, Sark lost to Gibraltar (19–0), Isle of Wight (20–0), Greenland (16–0) and Froya (15–0).

As the history of one-sided matches moves forward, so too does that of two-sided matches. This book already includes a match that ended 9–7 but that was replicated by Billington Synthonia's 9–7 win at Washington Nissan in the 2001–2 FA Carlsberg Vase. The match finished 6–6 after 90 minutes, and was poised at 8–7 before a last-minute goal by Ian Flanagan sealed the victory.

Another uncommon result was Weymouth's 8–5 win at Lewes in the FA Trophy in January 2004. Fans at the Lewes ground, known as the Dripping Pan, were spellbound as the goals kept going in. Weymouth led 3–2 after 20 minutes but Lewes equalised after 60 minutes. Then came seven more goals in the last half hour. Spectators debated among themselves how many Weymouth were ahead.

The Weymouth FC website put strangeness into perspective with the match report's final line: 'Incredibly this is not the first time Weymouth have won a match 8–5. The Terras recorded the same scoreline in a Dorset Senior Cup tie against Dorchester Town at the Rec on 3 December 1953.'

Anything can happen in football, and sometimes it can happen twice.

REFEREE SCORES WITH SUPERB VOLLEY

COLCHESTER, ESSEX, SEPTEMBER 2001

Put yourself in Brian Savill's place. You are refereeing a Colchester & District League match and Earls Colne Reserves are hammering Wimpole 18–1. You feel a little sorry for Wimpole.

It is a week after the terrorist attacks on New York City and Washington DC, and the mood is sombre. You are glad to be alive as you had a quadruple heart bypass operation almost exactly a year before. So you are looking for a way to celebrate life and cheer up everyone around you.

Then you see your chance.

Brian Savill's moment came ten minutes from the end of the game. A Wimpole player sent over a cross and the ball glanced off a defender towards the referee. Reacting on the spur of the moment, Savill raised his hand to stop the ball, then hit it sweetly on the volley with his left foot. The ball flew into the net and Savill awarded himself (and Wimpole) a goal.

There the fightback ended. The 12 men conceded two further goals and lost 20–2.

The incident was reminiscent of that created by dramatist Jack Rosenthal in a 1972 play called *Another Sunday and Sweet FA*. A referee is trying to control a match between two unruly local teams. He takes revenge by heading a goal for himself.

In Brian Savill's case, however, the critics were not

amused. The Essex County Football Association charged him with bringing the game into disrepute and suspended him for seven weeks. Savill immediately ended his 18-year refereeing career by resigning. He was disappointed that his county FA couldn't see the funny side of the matter. In return the Essex FA were disappointed to receive the resignation. They couldn't afford to lose referees.

34 CONSECUTIVE SHOOT-OUT GOALS

HECKMONDWIKE, DECEMBER 2001

The penalty shoot-out system was introduced to ensure a winner, but there isn't always a winner. When Littletown played Storthes Hall, the players took 34 penalty-kicks before bad light stopped play at 17–17. Several months later the *Guinness Book of Records* confirmed that 34 consecutive goals in a shoot-out was a world record.

The two teams were from the West Riding County Amateur Football League. They met on 29 December in a first-round Premier Division League Cup tie. The score was 1–1 after 90 minutes, and extra-time brought no further goals.

Then came the procession.

'Next?'

'Well done.'

'Next?'

'Great shot.' 'Next.'

'Next.'

'Next.'

… until the score was 17–17 and one goalkeeper, Liam Garside (Storthes Hall), had scored twice. Then failing light became a problem as there were no floodlights at the ground. Car-owners considerately switched on their headlights and the nearby street-lighting offered some help, but the ground eventually became so dark that one spectator described it as 'like playing down a pit'. The referee, Bob Hargreaves of Halifax, abandoned the match.

Only one question remained – how would they settle the tie? Toss a coin?

More penalties? A replay?

Straws? Corner-kicks? Golden goal? Silver goal?

In fact, the match was replayed four weeks later.

Other penalty shoot-outs might have involved more kicks but not without a player missing. Indeed, it was more likely to find shoot-outs at the other end of the hit-miss spectrum. For instance, a Derby Community Cup tie in 1998 brought together two teams of children under the age of ten. The kids battled through a 66-penalty shoot-out before one team won 2–1. The first 60 kicks were missed. The children must have been exhausted.

A month before the Littletown–Storthes Hall contest, a new FA Cup record had been set when Macclesfield won a first-round replay by beating Forest Green Rovers 11–10 on penalties after a 24-penalty shoot-out. Curiously, three penalties had been awarded during regulation time, making 27 for the tie.

For sheer success, though, Littletown and Storthes Hall moved to the top of the list.

MATCH ABANDONED – TOO FEW PLAYERS

SHEFFIELD, MARCH 2002

The Nationwide Division One match between Sheffield United and West Bromwich Albion was abandoned after 82 minutes when Sheffield United were reduced to six men. This created an English precedent. In the past, matches had only been abandoned because of adverse weather conditions, pitch invasions, crowd disasters, stadium fires, fatalities or serious injuries on the field, and when dismissed players had failed to depart the pitch.

On several occasions teams had *continued* with fewer than seven men – for instance, Manchester City in 1906, Chelsea in 1931 – but these were before the International Board's decision on the matter. In living memory, the Football Association has followed the Board's recommendation that 'a match should not be considered valid if there were fewer than seven players in either of the teams'.

On 16 March, West Brom were third in Division One, and Sheffield United were fifteenth. In-form Albion were 11 points behind the second automatic promotion spot (with a game in hand) and this was a critical period.

Ill-feeling had spilled over from the previous season, managers Neil Warnock (United) and Gary Megson (Albion) had been at loggerheads, and the atmosphere was highly charged. Police and stewards were involved before the match when an Albion fan ran on to the pitch and baited United supporters.

In the eighth minute United goalkeeper Simon Tracey was sent off after handling the ball several yards outside his penalty area as Scott Dobie lifted the ball over his head. United replaced a striker, Peter Ndlovu, with their deputy goalkeeper, Wilko de Vogt. Dobie headed West Brom into the lead in the eighteenth minute, and their captain Derek McInnes added a superb second in the sixty-second minute. A second Albion goal was strange in itself; 'one-nil to the Albion' was a contemporary catch-phrase.

With West Brom leading 2–0, Sheffield United manager Neil Warnock made two substitutions – Georges Santos for Michael Tonge and Patrick Suffo for Gus Uhlenbeek. The game immediately went out of control and both substitutes were sent off within minutes.

Santos renewed acquaintance with West Brom's midfielder Andy Johnson. A year previously Santos had spent five hours in surgery after fracturing a cheekbone in a collision with Johnson (then playing for Nottingham Forest). Now Santos made a terrible two-footed jump at Johnson. Santos was sent off and the injured Johnson had to be restrained by the physiotherapist and team-mates while still receiving treatment. Johnson limped off the field.

In the rumpus that followed, Suffo, the other substitute, head-butted McInnes with the referee nearby. Suffo was sent off, McInnes later had four stitches in the cut, and United were now down to eight.

Sheffield United captain Keith Curle, cautioned for a foul, then seemed to play as though he was seeking a second yellow card. But what stopped the match was two players departing the field with injuries.

By the time Michael Brown left the field, after 78 minutes, West Brom were 3–0 ahead, Dobie having added his second goal. Then Rob Ullathorne departed, and United's complement had fallen below the required seven. The referee, Eddie Wolstenholme, then made the correct decision to abandon the match after 82 minutes. His only alternative option was to call for a temporary suspension of play to see if one of United's injured players could return.

Derek McInnes refused to press criminal charges against Suffo when routinely asked by South Yorkshire Police. Five days after the match West Brom were awarded the three points. As Wolves had lost at home to lowly Grimsby Town, the momentum had swung towards West Brom, who went on to achieve automatic promotion.

Sheffield United later faced a number of charges from the Football Association. The club were fined £10,000 for failing to ensure that their players conducted themselves in an orderly manner. Manager Neil Warnock was cleared of a charge of improper conduct but he received a reprimand and £300 fine for his behaviour towards the fourth official. Suffo received a three-game suspension and £3,000 fine (on top of a three-match ban for the sending-off) and Santos would miss six matches altogether (four for the sending-off plus two more). Keith Curle received a two-match ban and £500 fine.

While Sheffield United–West Bromwich Albion was a precedent in English football, such abandonments had happened elsewhere, even in representative football: six Ecuador players were sent off in a 1977 international against Uruguay, and the match was abandoned at 1–1; the 2001 Angola–Portugal match was terminated when Angola were reduced to six (four sent off and one injured); five Rhodes players were sent off against Guernsey in the 2003 Island Games; and the 1992 Ethiopia–Morocco match in Rabat was abandoned after 65 minutes because the Ethiopians were down to six players. In the latter case, Ethiopia had had difficulty in fielding a team because six players had allegedly defected during an airport stopover in Italy. Ethiopia took the field with two goalkeepers in central defence and a 40-year-old coach in midfield.

In England, a 1999–2000 Worthington Cup tie between Millwall and Ipswich Town had been a close-run thing.

Millwall had two players dismissed and then lost three to injuries after using all their permitted substitutions. On that occasion the referee consulted with the manager of six-man Millwall and an injured player was brought back on.

149 OWN-GOALS

TOAMASINA, MADAGASCAR, OCTOBER 2002

A scoreline of 149–0 looks like it belongs in a one-sided cricket match, but it also occurred when the Stade Olympique l'Emyrne (SOE) soccer team staged a protest by scoring 149 own-goals and losing 149–0 to AS Adema.

The SOE players were angry about a refereeing decision in their previous match, when they had conceded a last-kick equaliser to a disputed late penalty. That 2–2 draw, against Domoina Soavina Atsimondrano, meant that AS Adema had won the Championship. The final match was no longer a showdown between SOE and AS Adema with the title at stake. The title was settled by a mini-league in which the top four teams played each other over an 11-day period. Before the final game, with the title decided, the SOE coach organised the protest. Everyone was amazed when his players passed the ball to each other from the kick-off and scored the first own-goal. On and on it went, own-goal after own-goal, until the referee did well to keep count. Angry spectators converged on the ticket-booths to demand refunds. One SOE player scored 69 own-goals, making him a real contender for the golden own-goal boot.

There have been games where three accidental own-goals have been scored in a match, but deliberate own-goals are very rare. Players may have scored an own-goal when trying to lose a match on purpose. It has also been suggested that a deliberate own-goal might be a way to balance an unfair goal, such as Arsenal's second against Sheffield United in 1999. Dennis Evans (Arsenal) deliberately kicked the ball into his own net at the end of a 1955 match against Blackpool at Highbury, but only because he thought he had heard the full-time whistle and was celebrating a 4–0 victory. A few moments later Arsenal won 4–1.

Certain rules provoke players into planning own-goals. One example occurred in the Thailand–Indonesia Tiger Cup match of 1998. Both teams wished to finish second to avoid favourites Vietnam in the next round. With a few minutes left, the score at 2–2, Indonesia attacked their own goal. Despite fervent defence by Thailand, Indonesia's goalkeeper got hold of the ball and threw it into his own net. The authorities punished the teams involved.

An even stranger example occurred in the 1994 Shell Caribbean Cup. The rules stipulated that drawn group matches would be decided by Golden Goals. More interestingly, an extra-time winning goal would count double in the for-and-against columns.

In the preliminary round, Group 1 consisted of Barbados, Puerto Rico and Grenada. Puerto Rico beat Barbados 1–0 on 23 January, and two days later Grenada beat Puerto Rico 1–0 with a Golden Goal which counted double.

When Barbados met Grenada on 27 January, Barbados had to beat Grenada by at least two goals to win the group and qualify for the next round. Barbados led 2–0 until the eighty-third minute when Grenada scored a crucial goal. Then, with a few minutes to play, Barbados realised that they could score an own-goal to take the match into sudden-death overtime, and then score a proper goal which would count double. After scoring an own-goal, however, they had an awkward few minutes while defending at both ends of the pitch. A goal at either end would have taken Grenada through.

In overtime, Barbados won the game 3–2 and as this counted as 4–2 they pipped Grenada on goal difference. So Barbados went through after scoring a deliberate own-goal.

UK POLITICIANS TAKE ON IRAQ

LONDON, MAY 2004

As the Iraqi people faced an uncertain future after the overthrow of Saddam Hussein, a team of UK politicians played the full Iraq national team in Chelsea. The match was arranged by Truce International, an organisation promoting peace and global unity through football. Truce International was founded in September 2003, inspired by the Christmas Day truce of 1914.

Football supporters talk flippantly about the torture of following certain teams – Manchester City comes to mind – but the Iraq international players literally had faced torture during the Saddam Hussein regime. Uday Hussein, Saddam's eldest son, had routinely used sadistic tactics if Iraq didn't win. Players had been flogged with electric cable, forced to climb a 66-ft (20-m) ladder and jump into a bath of raw sewage, sprayed with freezing water, or beaten on the soles of their feet. Some were blindfolded and placed in solitary confinement. Others were threatened with having their legs amputated and thrown to hungry dogs.

Considering the Iraqi people's suffering from other causes – the 1991 Gulf War, depleted uranium with its associated cancers and birth defects, United Nations sanctions, etc. – it is astonishing that their football team reached forty-fourth in the 2004 FIFA rankings, a higher position than Scotland, Wales and Northern Ireland. They drew with Uzbekistan and Palestine in World Cup qualifiers, and won their Olympic qualifying group to seal a place in the Athens tournament. All Iraq home matches were played in Jordan.

The Iraq national team was invited to Britain to play three matches: Trinidad & Tobago (at West Brom), an FA XI (at Macclesfield), opponents more appropriate to their standing, and a team of working politicians.

The Parliamentarians' 26-man squad consisted of 16 Labour MPs, three Labour Co-op MPs, six researchers and one Conservative MP. Their manager described his players as two goalkeepers and 24 defenders. Unfortunately he couldn't put them all on the pitch at the same time.

After photographs had been taken, the teams held a minute's silence in respect for those who had died in Iraq.

Then came the match. The politicians did much better than had been expected ... for about 15 minutes. Then Iraq scored the first of their 11 goals. Excellent goalkeeping by Alan Whitehead (Labour, Southampton Test) kept the score down, and the referee mercifully ended a match of many substitutions after 25 minutes of the second half. The score was 11–0 and the politicians were lucky to get nil.

Football matches have often been staged as an encouraging sign of normality (if there is any such thing in the aftermath of war). There were liberation games in Europe in 1945 and 1946. In November 1945, while Moscow Dynamo toured Britain, a British Army of the Rhine (BAOR) team visited Warsaw to play two matches against a Poland XI. BAOR won both and presented the Warsaw Football Association with two footballs (in short supply) and several Scottish jumpers.

A team representing the United Nations Protection Force (UNPROFOR) played against Red Star (Belgrade) in 1994. And in February 2002, a group of Afghan players called Kabul United played a team from the International Security and Assistance Force (ISAF) in what was called The Game of Unity. The venue, Ghazi Stadium, had been used to stage public executions until the overthrow of the Taliban government earlier that year. ISAF won 3–1.

THE GAME OF 25 HALVES
READING, SEPTEMBER 2004

In a game of 25 halves Trevor McDonald's XI beat the Elstead Village Idiots by a cricket score – 197 to 69 – and it needed a cricket scorer to keep count. On the sidelines Mary Clotworthy kept a tally of the goals and goalscorers.

The match kicked off at 1p.m. on Saturday 25 September and ended at 2p.m. the following day. During those 25 hours the players developed a routine of playing a 45-minute 'half' and then resting for 15 minutes. The breaks weren't so much half-time intervals as four-percentile respites.

The venue was the Clayfield Copse Recreation ground in Caversham Park Road. The players aimed to raise money for Comic Relief while posting a *Guinness Book of World Records* benchmark for the longest-ever football match. The 25 players ranged in age from 14 to 42. To qualify for the marathon they needed a doctor's certificate to prove their fitness. First-aid was present at the ground, and lots of water for the players to drink. The floodlights were switched on during the hours of darkness.

There were three injuries during the match so resources were stretched. One player had to continue for 11 hours. Others did their best to get some sleep on the sidelines while the match went on and on and on and on. By the end some players could hardly walk. Afterwards organiser Daniel Lewis claimed that he was planning to set another record – for the longest-ever sleep.

'DODGY LASAGNE'

LONDON, MAY 2006

The term 'dodgy lasagne' entered football folklore after
the last day of the 2005–6 Premiership season. Tottenham
Hotspur's final match was at West Ham United. A win would
guarantee Spurs fourth place, a spot they had held since
December, and qualification for the UEFA Champions
League. Fifth-place Arsenal wanted to win their last match,
at home to Wigan Athletic, and hoped for a Spurs slip-up.

A party of over 20 Spurs players were booked into the five-
star Marriott Hotel in east London. The players arrived at
7p.m. and soon afterwards enjoyed a buffet supper in one of
the hotel's private rooms. The Spurs nutritionist had been
consulted on the content of the meal and all seemed well
until the early hours of the morning. Then a number of
players were taken ill. At 5a.m. Spurs manager Martin Jol
was woken up by a phone call from the club doctor saying
that seven of his players had upset stomachs. No other
hotel guests seemed affected.

At 11.15a.m. a Spurs official talked to the hotel general
manager. The police were called in, and Tower Hamlets
council's health and safety department was informed.
About 20 police officers arrived around 12.30p.m. and
forensic scientists took away samples of food. By now lots of
rumours were spreading around the city. The chief rumour
was that the ill players had all eaten lasagne from the buffet.
Some informants said that not all the ill players had eaten

lasagne. Reporters identified a whole smorgasbord of food available in the Spurs buffet – pasta, salad, chicken, steak and so on.

At noon Spurs requested a postponement or a delayed kick-off in order to allow the players more time to recover. The Premier League said 'No' to a postponement as Spurs clearly had enough fit players on the books to fulfil the fixture and could call up replacements for such a local fixture. The police were against any extended delay because soccer fans were already drinking in pubs and too much drinking time was dangerous. A two-hour delay was offered but Spurs officials felt the players needed more time than that to recover.

Tottenham officials also knew that failing to fulfil the fixture would have serious consequences – Middlesbrough had been deducted three points in 1996–7 for failing to play at Blackburn and the punishment had ultimately cost the club relegation – so at 1.25p.m. everyone agreed that the match would start on time. Police accompanied the Spurs players on the journey to the stadium.

It was one of Tottenham's worst performances of the season. A number of players looked below par and illness offered an obvious explanation. Carl Fletcher gave West Ham a ninth-minute lead but Jermain Defoe equalised before half-time. Meanwhile Arsenal had gone 2–1 behind to Wigan before levelling at 2–2 by half-time. If both matches stayed level then Spurs would keep fourth place.

Spurs goalkeeper Paul Robinson kept Spurs in the game by saving a penalty kick by West Ham's Teddy Sheringham early in the second half. After Arsenal had taken the lead against Wigan Yossi Benayoun scored a late winner for West Ham. Arsenal went on to win 4–2, Spurs lost 2–1, and Arsenal took the last Champions League place. And it was all down to a 'dodgy lasagne'.

Or was it?

In fact the Health Protection Agency and Tower Hamlets Council environmental officers eventually agreed that food poisoning was not the likely explanation. The probable cause was an outbreak of a form of gastroenteritis called norovirus. Tests on the players showed that one player had a form of gastroenteritis that could have spread to the other players. The Marriott Hotel was thus exonerated.

In the ten days before the test results materialised the rumour grew stronger. The term 'dodgy lasagne' entered football vocabulary as a symbol of something that goes wrong with preparations and affects the participants. In the way that the expression 'sick as a parrot' gives parrots an unfair reputation – some species of parrot can outlive humans – so does 'dodgy lasagne' give the hotel business a bad name. But conspiracy theories live on to this day.

THE MATCH IN THE RIVER
BOURTON-ON-THE-WATER,
GLOUCESTERSHIRE, AUGUST 2007

Footballers wade crab-style through 6in (15cm) of water as they chase the ball towards the riverbank, kicking up spray and splashing spectators in the front rows. A player flicks the ball out of the water with his foot and volleys it upstream. The men wrestle with each other as they set off again.

This is the annual football match in the river at Bourton-on-the-Water, a town known as 'the Venice of the Cotswolds'. The River Windrush runs through the centre of Bourton-on-the-Water. Normally the river bubbles like a tame stream but in July 2007 it burst its banks. The High Street green turned into a lake and a hundred homes and businesses were flooded. Bourton-on-the-Water became 'Bourton-in-the-Water' or 'Bourton-under-Water'.

In the context of Gloucestershire's biggest-ever peacetime emergency – 48,000 homes lost electricity for two days, and about 350,000 people in the county were without mains drinking water for much longer – it was amazing that a match was played in the River Windrush five weeks after the floods. But the Bourton-on-the-Water river football match is one of Gloucestershire's great traditions – others include cheese rolling and woolsack racing – and the show must go on.

The players were mostly from Bourton Rovers, a Gloucestershire Northern Senior League team. The 'pitch' for the 2007 match was set up between the two bridges in the town centre. In the game's early days the bridges acted as goalframes. In modern times portable goals are put in the river in front of the bridges.

Nearly a hundred people congregated on each bridge. Those at the front dangled their legs off the edge. Hundreds of other spectators lined the riverbanks to watch the big match and some hung out of the windows of nearby houses. Children paddled in the water directly behind the goals. It was Bourton Rovers' largest attendance of the season and collectors went round with buckets.

The referee started the 2007 match by kicking the ball up in the air and the raucous scene was under way. Players were soon deliberately splashing each other and jostling like kids in a swimming pool. When one player did an orchestrated belly-flop in front of the referee he was shown a yellow card for diving. He wasn't the first person to have dived in a river.

Regular spectators in the front row of the riverbank knew to wear waterproof clothing and carry umbrellas. Others screamed and shrieked when hit by a spray of water. Tourists captured the scene with their cameras. Players shouted instructions to each other and a lot of energetic water fights took place away from the ball. The goals fell over a couple of times.

A wild clearance sent the ball into the crowd.

'Keep the ball in the river.'

The goalposts were so close to the riverbank that it was relatively easy to send the ball into the goalmouth from a throw-in. Players from both teams lurked in front of the smaller-than-normal goals as the ball looped through the air. Heading the ball was a relief after trying to kick it.

The rules of the Bourton match are not dissimilar to those of swamp soccer, a sport played on a pitch that has been rotavated and then soaked with hundreds of gallons of water. Swamp soccer and river football are both six-a-side games that rely on determination, energy and strength rather than raw football talent. In both codes the players take penalty-kicks and free-kicks by dropping the ball from their hands on to a favoured foot. Whereas the Bourton river game began in 1894, the year Bourton Rovers were founded, swamp soccer has a much shorter history, starting in 1997 when a group of cross-country skiers in Finland discovered that playing soccer in a swamp was a fun way of building up leg muscles in training. Also, the names of swamp-soccer teams are more inventive. The swamp-soccer World Championship features teams such as Real Mudrid, Cowdungbeath, Inter the Mud and Dirt Kuyt FC.

Water matches take a heavy physical toll. A 30-minute match in the River Windrush leaves players' feet feeling like ice, even on a hot August day. Players will tell you that 30 minutes of playing in the river is harder than 90 minutes on land. And swapping shirts is physically challenging. Getting them off your back is hard work. Then comes the wringing out.

In 2007, in the River Windrush, the Reds missed a penalty-kick but beat the Whites 2–1 before celebrating wildly and wetly with a sing-song in the river. The following year the riverbanks were strengthened against the possibility of further flood.

POSTPONED

ALTRINCHAM, DECEMBER 2008

Most football fans have woken up on a Saturday morning, seen the inclement weather and asked themselves 'Will the match be on?'

In modern times supporters monitor pitch inspections through Internet sites, fans forums, weather forecasts and mobile-phone interchanges. In some cases, however, fans have to set off so early that they face a journey into the unknown.

Simon Hood decided to travel by bicycle to every York City League and FA Cup match during the 2008–9 season. His chances of postponements while he was travelling were much higher than for most fans, because his journeys took longer. In December 2008 he had two long trips with no football at the end.

On the morning of the match between Grays Athletic and York City, Hood woke up in a friend's house in Ealing, London, where he had broken his journey from York. During the morning the Grays website was confident of the match being on, calling for supporters with 'small tractors or quad bikes' to help clear the snow off the pitch. At 11a.m. the pitch was playable; at noon the referee was not so sure.

Simon Hood set off anyway, but ran into trouble in Acton.

'The elasticated strap that held all the gear on top of the panniers together pinged off straight into the chainset, where it wedged itself,' he wrote in his book *Bicycle Kicks*.

'The sharp stop caused me to fall onto the pavement, to the pedestrians' annoyance.'

Hood set off to find a bike shop and, at 1p.m., learned that the match was on and he'd probably miss it. Fifteen minutes later the match was called off.

Later in the month he watched a match at York on Boxing Day and immediately afterwards set off for Altrincham, south of Manchester, for a 3p.m. kick-off on 28 December. The first leg of the journey took him to Wetherby, where he stayed the night with his brother. The next day he cycled through the snow-covered Pennines and stayed the night in Wharfedale. On 28 December he got as far as Rochdale before he learned the Altrincham match was postponed.

Weather is the most likely cause of postponement but football history has thrown up other strange reasons – players' strikes (usually for unpaid wages), unsafe grandstands, epidemics, floodlight failures, security threats, dog mess on the pitch, toxic fumes from a nearby fire and the destruction of a pitch by a flock of geese.

One of the most ironic postponements was the inability of staff, players and fans to travel to through the snow to the all-weather pitch at Queen's Park Rangers. Some of the strangest matches are those that never take place.

BEACH BALL SCORES WINNING GOAL

SUNDERLAND, OCTOBER 2009

Five minutes of the match between Sunderland and Liverpool had gone when Sunderland's Steed Malbranque ran down the right wing and centred the ball. Darren Bent met the cross with a low right-foot shot from 15 yards (13.7m). Confusion followed.

Liverpool goalkeeper Pepe Reina looked to have the ball covered but a big red beach ball was resting on the 6-yard line in front of Reina's goal. The match ball cannoned off the beach ball and flew past Reina's left side. Reina had instinctively moved to his right, towards the beach ball, only to see it go past the post. The match ball lay snugly inside the net.

Referee Mike Jones talked to his assistant and gave a goal.

One-nil to Sunderland.

The Liverpool fans were behind Reina's goal. Before the match they had been playing with the red beach ball (with a Liverpool crest), cheerily hitting it to each other, until a 16-year-old Liverpool fan at the front of the crowd knocked the ball on to the pitch. Reina had retrieved the beach ball and put it behind him but it drifted back out on to the pitch, where it received a solid thump from the match ball after Bent's shot.

As the game continued Sunderland went close to extending their lead and Bent could have scored a hat-trick. But Sunderland goalkeeper Craig Gordon had to make two good saves near the end to preserve his team's 1–0 lead. At the end of the match Liverpool fans were deflated. If only the beach ball had been deflated too.

The referee got the law wrong and made the wrong decision. The laws of football state that the correct decision should have been 'no goal' and play restarted with a dropped ball. Whenever an outside agent or foreign object is on the field, play should be stopped and resumed with a dropped ball. That is what should have happened.

The two managers and all the players had no idea that the decision was wrong. Morally, a Liverpool fan had been to blame so justice was done in one way. By the laws of football, however, there was a case for replaying the match because the referee had got the law wrong and refereeing error of that kind (technical error) could be punished by a replay. It had probably been too long since Mike Jones had refereed in local parks, where this sort of thing happened more often. The next week Jones was demoted and put in charge of a Championship match between Peterborough United and Scunthorpe United.

Over the years football pitches have been littered with objects thrown by spectators. We have seen bottles, beer cans, plastic coffee cups, leeks, cutlery, ball bearings, toilet rolls, cigarette lighters, coins, darts, balloons, meat pies, hot dogs, snooker balls, artificial limbs and mobile phones. A stuffed pig's head was once thrown at Luis Figo of Real Madrid, and an FA Cup tie between Burton Albion and Leicester City was replayed after Burton goalkeeper Paul Evans had been hit by a piece of wooden seating.

Under the Football (Offences) Act 1991, throwing an object towards the playing area (or towards other spectators) is an offence unless there is a lawful excuse (with the onus on the accused to prove it). Meanwhile, the best place for a beach ball is on the beach.

ILLOGAN RBL RESERVES 55 MADRON FC 0

ILLOGAN, CORNWALL, NOVEMBER 2010

With the minimum of seven players and no recognised goalkeeper Madron FC travelled 20 miles (32.2km) from Penzance to the Illogan RBL ground, near Redruth. Madron were bottom of the Cornwall Mining League Division One and Illogan RBL Reserves were top. The difference in numbers and class showed somewhat in the 55–0 scoreline, a UK record for an adult match. Thirty-one goals came in the second half.

Eleven different players scored for Illogan RBL at Oxford Parc that day. Luke Abbott-Smith hit ten, Gareth Pitt eight and Luke Helan seven. Three other players – Ryan Treloar, Jason Buckley and Mikey Pascoe – bagged double hat-tricks.

Newly promoted Madron were in a sorry state as they had suffered an exodus of players at the start of the season. This 55-goal defeat to Illogan Reserves, in the Cornwall Mining League Division One, meant that Madron had now conceded 205 goals in the first ten matches of their season. They had scored only one goal.

The story was that a number of Madron first teamers had been called in to work and two players cried off with injury. Meanwhile, the Madron second team had 13 players available for their home match in Division Three and they beat Redruth Reserves 6–2.

The next week Madron showed considerable improvement when they lost 22–0 at St Buryan. By the end of their

28-match season the Madron first team had conceded 407 goals and scored only 12. Their heavy defeats included being thrashed twice by Gwinear Churchtown – 27–1 at home and 24–0 away – and a 27–0 hammering at home to Trevenson United. Madron's goal difference of minus 395 could have worse as they lost one match by a walkover. Needless to say it was a case of no points and deserved relegation.

WHEEL POWER FC 58
NOVA 2010 FC 0
TORBAY, DEVON, MARCH 2012

Sixteen months after Illogan Reserves had thrashed Madson 55–0, the feat was bettered by Wheel Power FC, a club based in the Torbay area. Wheel Power beat Nova 2010 FC 58–0 in a Torbay Sunday League mismatch.

Only five Nova 2010 players showed up but frantic phone calls produced another three. The match was soon a story of a confident home side trouncing a short-handed team of disheartened players. Wheel Power scored 20 in the first half and 38 in the second.

One spectator said that Wheel Power could have scored 70 with better finishing, and a Wheel Power player reckoned the referee's Biro had gone blunt from recording goals in his notebook. A Nova 2010 player said, 'We expected to lose but not by that much.'

Some Wheel Power players had played at a much higher level. Take Robbie Bowker for instance. On Saturdays he played for Liverton United in the South West Peninsular League. A roofer from Torbay, Bowker was obviously good on the air … and not too bad on the ground. In the match against Nova 2010, Bowker scored 18 and his brother Stuart smashed home ten goals. There can't be many cases of two brothers scoring 28 goals in a game between them. In that same season Robbie Bowker scored 16 in a 30–0 victory against Appleby.

Perhaps the most astonishing thing, though, was that

Wheel Power scored 38 goals in the second half. Top-level footballers can waste 30 or 40 seconds celebrating a goal. Maybe Wheel Power players, scoring a goal every 70 seconds, had little new to say to say to each other after they reached 20-odd goals.

GOALIE SENT OFF ...
AGAIN AND AGAIN AND
AGAIN

OXFORD AND ELSEWHERE, JANUARY AND FEBRUARY 2015

Perhaps Oxford City's bad luck with goalkeepers started the previous year, in January 2014, when regular City goalie Victor Francoz was injured. Mike Ford, the Oxford City manager at that time, was unimpressed with Francoz's injury. Apparently the 23-year-old goalkeeper was climbing a tree trying to rescue a distressed cat when he fell off and suffered a deep gash in his calf.

A year later new Oxford City manager Justin Merrett faced another goalkeeping crisis. Merrick's team were chasing promotion to the Vanarama Conference but his goalkeepers kept being sent off. It happened four times in 29 days, starting with the match at home to Barrow on Saturday 24 January.

The first-choice goalkeeper was Salva de la Cruz, who had played for the Spain Under-17 team earlier in his career. Salva, as he was known in football circles, had been with City for nearly two months. But he was sent off in the sixth minute of the Barrow game after Barrow's Karl Ledsham had gone down in the penalty area. There was no substitute goalkeeper on the bench so outfield player Darren Pond, the team's captain and central defender, deputised in goal for almost the whole match. Barrow won 3–0 and Oxford City unsuccessfully appealed against the sending-off.

After a 1–0 defeat at Worcester City, when Mark Scott deputised in goal, Salva was back in the Oxford City team for the home match against Tamworth. Adi Yussuff put City ahead in the fifty-third minute. Immediately afterwards Salva handled the ball outside the penalty area and was sent off. Declan Benjamin switched from midfielder to goalkeeper and kept a clean sheet in the 1–0 win.

City's next Vanarama Conference North match, at Brackley Town, started with Mark Scott in goal ... but only until the thirty-ninth minute. The goalkeeper seemed to have beaten David Moyo to a loose ball but the referee viewed it differently and brought out the red card. City were 1–0 up at the time, and Scott seemed shocked that he was being sent off. Oxford City had no substitute goalkeeper on the bench, so midfielder Declan Benjamin took over again. A Brackley player was sent off midway through the second half – it became a ten-a-side match – and City went on to win 5–0. It was Benjamin's second clean sheet.

A week later Oxford City beat Lowestoft Town 2–1 with Salva in goal and Scott serving a ban. Both Salva and Scott would miss the next match, at Tamworth, but manager Justin Merritt was delighted to make the loan signing of Ali Aksoy, a Turkish goalkeeper who had played for AFC Wimbledon. There was no back-up goalkeeper on the bench – it was hard finding one goalkeeper let alone two – and you can guess what happened. Yes, five minutes after half-time, with City leading 3–2, goalkeeper Aksoy sprinted out of goal, brought down Tamworth's Hibbert and was sent off. Declan Benjamin took over yet again. This time he conceded two goals and Tamworth won 4–3.

After the match manager Merritt spoke about the run of bad luck: 'They say lightning doesn't strike twice but it's four times now.'

A PAIR OF BROKEN ARMS
SCUNTHORPE, JANUARY 2015

Oxford City manager Justin Merrett wasn't the only one searching for replacement goalkeepers that January; Scunthorpe United manager Mark Robins was doing the same. Two Scunthorpe United goalkeepers suffered broken arms in the first half of a home match against Bristol City.

Once upon a time, in the middle of the twentieth century, goalkeepers suffered buffetings in all sorts of ways – dubious shoulder charges, diving at players' feet, etc. – and they faced serious injury or even death. Gradually the laws of the game were tightened so that goalkeepers were given more protection. By the start of the twenty-first century goalkeepers were receiving only 60 per cent of the injuries of outfield players.

Scunthorpe United were unbeaten in seven matches when they hosted promotion-chasing Bristol City. The crowd wasn't particularly big – 3,611 – but it proved to be vociferous, especially after the goalkeepers were injured.

Sam Slocombe, a Scunthorpe man, was the Iron's starting goalkeeper. In the tenth minute a cross from the left wing saw Slocombe punch the ball away from a crowded goal area while colliding with Bristol City's Matt Smith. The goalkeeper was holding his left arm in obvious discomfort. He walked towards the halfway-line, grimacing, aware he couldn't continue.

Slocombe was replaced by 23-year-old James Severn,

wearing shirt number 13. In over three years at Scunthorpe Severn had made one start, when he'd saved a penalty against Portsmouth.

Scunthorpe had the better of the first half but Bristol City were awarded a penalty kick in the thirty-fifth minute. Jay Emmanuel-Thomas took the slowest-ever run-up, from outside the penalty area to the penalty spot, before placing a low left-foot kick past goalkeeper James Severn's right hand.

A few minutes later the injury hoodoo struck again. Severn came out to dive at the feet of Matt Smith and, after making the save, lay still on the ground. The game continued for some seconds and Emmanuel-Thomas was about to attempt a long-range shot into an empty net when the referee blew the whistle for the injury. Severn, down on the floor, received treatment for several minutes.

Scunthorpe central defender Andy Boyce, the nearest player to Severn, immediately decided that he would go in goal in the absence of another specialist goalkeeper. He told the team's captain that he'd played in goal before – when he was nine or ten playing on small pitches – and he became the third keeper of the half.

Boyce put on a green jersey and wore it outside his claret shorts rather than tucked in. He punched one clear and caught a corner cleanly, clutching it to his chest for safety. He saved with his feet from Emmanuel-Thomas but conceded a goal by Luke Freeman near the end of the match. Bristol City won 2–0.

After the match Scunthorpe manager Mark Robins said: 'We've lost two goalkeepers in this game to the same injury – broken arms under a challenge from one of their players. I'm disappointed for them because they've broken their arms. I'm disappointed for the players because I thought we were the better team on the day, and I'm extremely disappointed with the decisions of the referee, or non-decisions of the referee.'

Robins knew that Slocombe and Severn would be out of action for three months, so he brought in two more goalkeepers – Luke Daniels (from West Brom) and Joe Anyon (from Crewe Alexandra). The two injured goalkeepers travelled to London for surgery on their fractured arms.

THE PICK-UP GAME
CAMBRIDGE, EVERY SATURDAY AND TUESDAY

The pick-up game is still alive and kicking. Soccer has not lost its evolutionary charm. Such games do not necessarily take place in streets or back-alleys now, but people still meet informally on some small patch of land, divide into roughly even sides, adapt rules if necessary and do their best to maintain some sort of justice without an official referee.

In the late 1970s and early 1980s I played regularly in a reliable pick-up game started by members of King's College, Cambridge. It was a motley collection of people, men and women, classicists, overseas students, labourers, milkmen, cartoonists and so on. We would meet at some approximate time, decide on the latest fad for picking sides – those in white shirts down that end, size nines against the rest, Britain against the Rest of the World – and start when enough people were ready. Predicting who would arrive late was part of the skill of choosing teams.

There would usually be a debate about rules. In my time we played with small goals – their goal was always smaller than ours – and no players allowed to handle the ball. Goals were allowed only if the ball went along the ground from less than 4 yards (3.7m) out, although headers and own-goals could be scored from anywhere on the pitch. The size of the pitch varied, depending on how many were playing and whose arguments were accepted.

In the depths of winter, playing with dwindling numbers, more invention was needed. If the numbers were odd we would play around one goal, one team playing into the back of the goal, the other into the front. The goal-line doubled as a halfway-line. The one goalkeeper would be constantly turning around, depending on which team was attacking. This game, of course, can work only if there are no nets.

One day there were seven of us in the snow. There was no obvious four against three team selection, but the Australian among us had a brainwave: we would start with four against three and then anyone scoring a goal would switch to the other side. This seemed very fair in theory. In practice, after ten minutes or so, I found myself 2–0 up and on my own against six of them, wondering who I wanted to score. But it was fun thinking it through, as it is with all novelty matches. Only when a game is established is the participant's choice restricted. Sometimes the discovery of one tactic destroys the fun of invention.

A Second Division team once experimented in training with a two-ball practice-match. The idea was that the players would sharpen up their reactions and vision because twice as much would be happening. Instead, a trio of experienced defenders killed the game when they discovered the tactic of keeping one ball in a boring triangle while their forwards played with the other.

Children, however, retain the spirit of invention. Recently I happened upon four boys playing two-a-side soccer on a disused northern tennis-court. I stopped and watched for almost five minutes as one side attacked ferociously and the other team defended heroically. Then a couple of quick passes and a ricochet and the attacking team were through to score. The scorer leapt in the air, twirled his arms, scaled the wire fence and did a lap of honour. Ah, I thought, that's the goal they've been looking for. That's the breakthrough. That's the goal the commentator's been saying the game needed.

The goalscorer's team-mate took a break from celebrating to announce the score. 'Twenty-seven to us, 16 to you,' he said.

I walked away, thinking there was still hope for strange soccer matches.

OTHER TITLES IN

THE STRANGEST SERIES

The *Strangest* series has been delighting and enthralling readers for decades with weird, exotic, spooky and baffling tales of the absurd, ridiculous and the bizarre. This range of fascinating books – from Football to London, Rugby to Law and many subjects in between – details the very curious history of each one's funniest, oddest and most compelling characters, locations and events.

CRICKET'S STRANGEST MATCHES

9781910232910

GOLF'S STRANGEST ROUNDS

9781910232934

KENT'S STRANGEST TALES
9781910232972

LAW'S STRANGEST CASES
9781910232897

LONDON'S STRANGEST TALES
9781910232880

MEDICINE'S STRANGEST CASES
9781910232941

MOTOR RACING'S STRANGEST RACES
9781910232965

RUGBY'S STRANGEST MATCHES
9781910232873

RUNNING'S STRANGEST TALES
9781910232927

SHAKESPEARE'S STRANGEST TALES
9781910232903

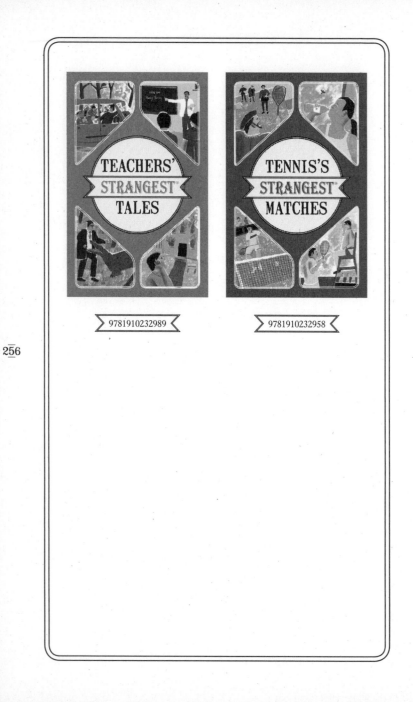

TEACHERS' STRANGEST TALES

9781910232989

TENNIS'S STRANGEST MATCHES

9781910232958